THE WARMUP GUY

THE WARMUP GUY

Bob Perlow
and Richard John Cummins
foreword by Alan Thicke

PELICAN PUBLISHING COMPANY
GRETNA 2016

The word "Pelican" and the depiction of a pelican are
trademarks of Pelican Publishing Company, Inc., and are
registered in the U.S. Patent and Trademark Office.

Library of Congress Cataloging-in-Publication Data

Perlow, Bob.
  The warmup guy / by Bob Perlow and Richard John Cummins ;
foreword by Alan Thicke.
     pages cm
  Includes index.
  ISBN 978-1-4556-2150-7 (hardcover : alk. paper) — ISBN
978-1-4556-2151-4 (e-book) 1. Perlow, Bob. 2. Comedians—
United States—Biography. 3. Television writers—United States—
Biography. 4. Actors—United States—Biography. I. Cummins,
Richard John, 1966- II. Title.
  PN2287.P3935A3 2016
  792.702'8092—dc23
  [B]

                                        2015036302

Printed in the United States of America
Published by Pelican Publishing Company, Inc.
1000 Burmaster Street, Gretna, Louisiana 70053

To my sister Judy: my angel, my confidante, and my most ardent supporter. I love you. And to Marc Sotkin, a good friend and mentor for more than forty years, who said in 1975: "So ya wanna be a writer on the No. 1 show on TV?" (Thank God he did.)

—B. P.

Contents

Foreword 9

Introduction 13

Chapter One: Life Before LA 17

Chapter Two: Bus Tours 23

Chapter Three: Laverne & Shirley 31

Chapter Four: Angie 45

Chapter Five: Mork & Mindy 53

Chapter Six: Taxi. 65

Chapter Seven: Cheers 73

Chapter Eight: Newhart 79

Chapter Nine: Oh, Madeline 91

Chapter Ten: Night Court 97

Chapter Eleven: People Do the Craziest Things. 105

Chapter Twelve: Night of the Comet 111

Chapter Thirteen: Growing Pains. 113

Chapter Fourteen: Full House 125

Chapter Fifteen: Who's the Boss?. 137

Chapter Sixteen: House Party with Steve Doocy 147

Chapter Seventeen: Let Bob Do It 153

Chapter Eighteen: The Rock and Roll Hall of Fame
    Induction Ceremony 165

Chapter Nineteen: Candid Camera 173

Chapter Twenty: Coach 185

Chapter Twenty-One: Home Improvement. 191

Chapter Twenty-Two: Jay Leno and The Tonight Show 195

Chapter Twenty-Three: Friends. 205

Chapter Twenty-Four: Scare Tactics 217

Chapter Twenty-Five: Dharma & Greg. 219

Chapter Twenty-Six: The Wrapup Guy. 223

Acknowledgments 227

Index. 231

Foreword

Bob Perlow is an acquired taste that once acquired is impossible to shake. His unique voice made him a legendary warmup guy—the prototype and one of the pioneers, in fact, of that job description.

He was never a "setup-and-joke" type but rather a comedic performance artist: a walking reality show who engages with the audience, improvising seamlessly with them until everyone is laughing—which never takes long with Bob.

As the opening act for dozens of TV stars, including Jay Leno, the first face a guest star saw in the studio hallway would be Bob's. And that charm and humor had to kick in immediately—so important in setting the tone for the on-air hilarity to follow.

In that role, a nosy person can't help but collect a wealth of stories, opinions, and gossip (OK, dirt!) about the hundreds of A-listers with whom he has worked. Now that he's willing to share that fly-on-the-wall insider's perspective—watch out!

I have been privileged to know Bob as more than a biographer/tattletale to the stars. He is a longtime family friend who's been there with a camera—an occasionally annoying habit of his—for important moments such as the exact day my son Robin became taller than me, then when the same happened with my younger son Carter.

He was the court jester, the weird uncle at family gatherings. He was my wingman when I was between relationships (or between series), when I was too shy (or too cancelled) to approach a pretty girl.

I have been a private audience to his celebrity anecdotes and shocking backstage revelations, and I highly recommend him to you in the same delicious capacity.

Thanks for including me in your *Growing Pains* section, Bob. I hope you said something nice or I will certainly take my foreword back.

Hop aboard for the Perlow Parade, a unique peek behind the scenes at Hollywood's television icons!

Alan Thicke
May 2015

Introduction

At this point in my life, I can almost predict exactly the way the conversation is going to go whenever I meet someone for the first time. It's usually something like this:

ME: Hello, I'm Bob.
THEM: Oh, hi. I'm Ed.
ME: What do you do?
THEM: Oh, I'm retired. What about yourself?
ME: I'm retired too. What did you do for a career?
THEM: I was an accountant. And you?
ME: I worked in television.
THEM: TV! Sounds exciting! What did you do exactly?
ME: A variety of things, actually. I was a writer, and an actor, but mainly I was a warmup guy.
THEM: [*very confused*] Writer, actor, and . . . warmup guy? What's that?

So you see what I'm up against. Such conversations would be quite a bit easier if I did have a career—like "accountant"—that can be explained with a single word.

Nonetheless, not having an easy-to-explain job is a small price to pay for getting to experience the exciting and fulfilling career that I've had.

With only a few exceptions, the job doesn't really even exist outside of Los Angeles. Beyond that, if you're either not in the business or have never been to the taping of a live TV show, you may not even be aware that there's such a thing as a "warmup guy" or "warmup comic" (the other common term).

So for those who may still be confused like my (hypothetical) buddy Ed, I will briefly explain what it is I did.

When a TV sitcom was being taped in front of a live studio audience, I was the only one essentially responsible for the audience once they were in their seats. Everyone else on the set, from the producers to the grips, had his or her own job, so I was the person designated to talk to the audience. They were stuck with me, and I with them. It was a blast.

I would introduce the show, and then while the taping was underway I would keep them entertained through a variety of methods (many of which I'll describe in the pages to come) during the breaks. And those breaks could be many, and they could be long—a taping could very well take up to six hours or more. For all that time I had to make sure that everyone stayed and (hopefully) still felt like laughing.

I would end up doing well over a thousand tapings, so I got to experience all of these shows from both sides of the fence, as both an insider and also as the spectator with the best imaginable vantage point.

Why write this book? I'm very much a child of TV. I consider myself more of a fan than anything else, a fan who just happened to have the good fortune of getting to work in the industry for thirty-five years and along the way build up an impressive collection of true stories about everyone's favorite TV shows and celebrities.

Some were great. Most were good. Some were bad. A few were really bad. But they all happened.

Enjoy!

THE WARMUP GUY

Chapter One

Life Before LA

As proud as I am of all my accomplishments, I also take a certain degree of satisfaction in something that I managed *not* to do. I did audience warmup for thirty-five years, which meant speaking to literally thousands of people, the vast majority of whom were tourists. However, I almost never tried to break the ice with any of them by asking where they were from.

I was never a fan of this approach to begin with. It's far too obvious. Also, too many comics, and event hosts, insist on using it as a set-up for that hackneyed routine we've all heard a million times: "Where are you from?" "Philadelphia." "I'm sorry?" "Philadelphia." "I heard you. I'm just *sorry*." Badda-boom.

What I've always wanted very much to do was to differentiate myself from everyone else who was doing audience warmup. Had producers heard me asking people that question, they might have immediately thought, "He's just like everyone else." And being "like everybody else" means that all of us are pretty interchangeable, which in turn means that any of us can be replaced.

Ironically, I don't mind anyone asking me where *I'm* from. The answer to that is Pawtucket, Rhode Island. I was born on December 28, 1945, making me among the first to arrive at the party known as the Baby Boomer generation. I am the youngest of three children and the only boy.

Both sets of my grandparents immigrated at the beginning of the 1900s as part of the massive wave of Russian Jews seeking refuge in the United States. My sisters and I were raised Jewish, but my family was always more culturally Jewish than religious.

My parents worked at a small local shoe store that my paternal grandfather had started. A man we called Uncle Charlie (we called him this because he was my uncle and his name was Charlie) had been made the owner because my father wasn't interested in dealing with the headache of overseeing the business. Although the store is now closed, today I can go to nearly any part of Rhode Island, and whenever people of a certain age hear my last name they automatically say, "Oh, yes! *Shoes!*" or "Oh, the shoe people!"

Our family got its first television set when I was about five years old. This was around 1951, and we only picked up three channels, none of which were even broadcasting around-the-clock. And what was on the screen was just as limited: there was lot of boxing and wrestling (not to mention more than a few test patterns, since programming typically ended fairly early in the day).

But the narrow selection of viewing choices never kept kids in my generation from staying glued to the TV. From almost the first flicker, parents all over America took full advantage of the new "electronic babysitter." My mother, who worked twelve hour days at the shoe store, was no exception.

Among my absolute favorites as a kid was *The Mickey Mouse Club*, the original version (i.e., not the one with Britney Spears and Justin Timberlake). Although my favorite segments of the show were the *Spin and Marty* serials, like almost all males my age my first crush was Annette Funicello. (And dreams do come true, as she and I would later appear together on an episode of *Full House*.)

Even though I eventually would have a successful career in TV comedy, I don't remember as a kid ever being particularly enamored of the groundbreaking work that people like Lucille Ball, Jackie Gleason, and Milton Berle were doing during the medium's early days (although I would certainly come to appreciate all of it as I got older). But my family never ever missed *The Ed Sullivan Show*. That was always our—and America's—Sunday night ritual.

Honestly, at no point did it ever enter my mind while I

was growing up that I even could, or would want to, work in television when I got older. It seemed too far from reality in my little Rhode Island to even be a dream.

After graduating from high school in 1963, I enrolled at the University of Rhode Island to major in business. The Vietnam War would escalate within a couple of years. A friend of mine who was serving over there ended up getting killed almost immediately after he arrived, and this was a story that was becoming typical for far too many of us during this period. I knew I did not want to have to end up going there myself. So, as there was a draft deferment for students, I just studied *slowly*.

I spent the summer between my sophomore and junior years living in Las Vegas. I was a short-order cook at the Stardust, one of the most renowned Vegas hotels of that era. (The venue and the atmosphere were very similar to what was later portrayed in the movie *Casino*.)

I was there on August 25, 1965. That was the day that President Johnson announced a deferment for any man who was married by midnight. Of course, since getting married in Vegas is pretty much as easy as buying a hooker—er . . . *newspaper*—thousands of couples fled there on that day, and within hours there were lines around the block at all of the many local wedding chapels.

Figuring it must have been kismet, since I had been in the city already, my girlfriend and I decided to get in one of the lines to get married ourselves. But the closer we got to the front of the line, the more we realized the impracticality of the idea, draft or no draft.

It's probably best that we didn't go through with it, since the marriage deferment only lasted a short time. (Not only that, it was altered to apply to men who were married *and had a child*, which I might have had a harder time getting her to go along with.)

Ultimately, I didn't even have to look for ways to be exempt from service—the government found most of them for me. I ended up being put through the military physical about five times, and it turned out I had a laundry list of 4-F classifications ranging from a hernia to the ever-popular flat feet. I pretty much felt fine, but of course I didn't tell *them* that.

Vietnam . . . not a great war.

Still, I didn't want to take any chances with the draft, so I remained in school in order to continue to qualify for that deferment. I stayed at the University of Rhode Island and started on my graduate studies just three weeks after getting my bachelor's degree. That was 1967.

Like most people, I was surprised at how fast the world was changing, even though I was part of the generation that was implementing the change. There were many anti-war protests on campus, a few of which inevitably turned violent. But it was an exciting time for someone to be in their twenties. I saw Cream and Jimi Hendrix perform live. I had coffee with Bob Dylan in Greenwich Village.

One time I attended a performance by Janis Joplin at Boston University. I was in the crowd right by the side of the stage as she started making her way up to do her set. We made eye contact, and she handed me the bottle of Southern Comfort that she had been holding. I took a swig and handed it back to her, after which she took a drink herself before finally walking back towards the stage.

Obviously I didn't end up the way Joplin, or a few too many members of my generation, did. However, without going into further detail, I can't honestly say that I avoided all of the era's more questionable common practices. (I admit: I inhaled . . . *everything*. And a lot!)

I became a teacher right after getting my master's degree, and a couple of years later I accepted an offer to become a professor at Chamberlain Junior College. This meant moving to Boston, which would be the first time I had ever lived outside of Rhode Island for an extended period of time.

While teaching—thankfully—continued to keep me out of Vietnam (my stance had not changed), several things happened to me in Boston that would have a profound effect on my life later on. First, I would get involved with improvisational comedy (which is usually referred to as simply "improv") for the first time. While doing that I would also become friends with a guy originally from upstate New York who was a bit younger than I was named James Douglas Muir Leno. He went by the nickname "Jay." (Much more on him later.)

I had been teaching in Boston for a few years when I got a call from another friend of mine who had been working on cruise ships based out of the Caribbean. He had been the cruise director on these lines but was spending a lot of his time, shall we say, "entertaining" some of the female passengers in a way that was not advertised in the brochures.

One of these women finally became so jealous that she claimed to the cruise line that he had stolen her jewelry. He was fired, not surprisingly, but still they allowed him to look for his own replacement (odd, huh?). He asked me if I might be interested in doing it.

For anyone who's never actually worked in the cruise ship industry, allow me to clear up two misconceptions that you probably formed from watching the ten-year run of *The Love Boat*. First of all, yes, there are male cruise directors as well as female. Second, there is not a wacky crew that is permanently assigned to a single ship. Most people who work on board end up servicing a variety of different ships.

In fact, after I took the job I didn't even work directly for the cruise line but rather for a travel company, which would rent the ships out and then set up cruises for various specific groups. One of the biggest clients was Zotos, the hair products company of the time that offered cruises as rewards to their most successful salespeople. I even worked on what may have been the first gay cruise ever commercially offered. (Since then it's become a cottage industry.)

After I had done this successfully for a couple of years, the company offered me a new job doing bus tours on the West Coast. I ended up flying out to California to start the new job on my thirtieth birthday. During the flight, I started thinking about the irony of not so much the date as the fact that I was going to be a tour guide for a city I had never even been to before.

The furthest thing from my mind, however, was the television industry. Of course, like everyone else, I knew that it was located in LA, which was my destination. But so were the La Brea Tar Pits, and I didn't think that that was going to have any bearing on my future either.

However, comedy would have to wait a couple of years. First I had to give some tours . . . although those themselves turned out to be a comedy of errors, as you'll find out in the next chapter. Read on.

Chapter Two

Bus Tours

The job that brought me to Los Angeles in 1975 was being a tour guide. The company was called, quite literally, Discount Travel. The name told you everything you needed to know. As the old adage goes, you get what you pay for (although actually, in this case you probably got even *less* than you paid for).

The tours lasted exactly two weeks. They would begin in Las Vegas, then go to Los Angeles, and end up in San Francisco, with stops in Yosemite and Monterey. The deal being offered was aimed mostly at lower-middle class clientele who lived on the East Coast and were—to put it cordially—on a budget. It was an entire package (including round-trip airfare from New York City) for a flat rate of about four hundred dollars.

Each tour group was composed of about ninety people. We would put them all on a flight from JFK airport in New York City to LA. As soon as they got off the plane, I would greet them and introduce myself as their tour guide. Then, bags transferred, we would split them up into two groups and put them right on a couple of buses . . . to Las Vegas.

It never took long for some of the people to openly question the logic of this route. Everyone knows Vegas is closer to New York than LA. So why not simply fly them right to Vegas from the East Coast instead of starting in LA and then having to double back?

Hard geography wasn't the only issue: These people had already just been through a very draining travel day, having to get on a flight early in the morning, to say nothing of everything that can and will go wrong with air travel. And now, after they had been on the ground for literally *minutes*, we were about to subject them to a four to five hour bus ride across the Mojave Desert.

The real reason was that it's less expensive to fly to LA from New York, even though Vegas is technically closer. (It costs more to land a charter plane in Vegas.) However, when asked, I always told them we were taking them on the bus ride because we wanted them to experience just how beautiful the desert would be during the time of day that we would be traveling.

It was complete crock, but of course I laid it all on as thick as I possibly could with a straight face: "To experience what Native Americans call *Chataga*, which means 'the beauty of the desert.'" (*Chataga*, of course, was a word that I made up.) Or I'd tell them, "I guarantee you'll never see anything like it in New York City!" "You'll always regret missing it!" etc.

All ninety or so people, as well as the drivers and myself, piled into the buses. Everyone inevitably wanted to sit as close to the front as possible. For one, they wanted the best view of where we were going. But more importantly, nobody wanted to sit near the toilet at the (appropriately named) rear of the bus. They could already tell how bad it started to smell on just this first day of the trip (and we had eleven more ahead of us) before it had even been used. And the scent was only that of disinfectant!

Sitting towards the front of the bus wasn't simply the preference—people became not just aggressive but actually violent over it. I would see fist-fights break out! I had no choice but to devise a rotation system, whereby everyone could take turns sitting in the more desirable seats.

But some people weren't satisfied with even that. On nearly every trip there would be at least one person who had obviously anticipated this scenario and went as far as to get a note from their doctor claiming that they couldn't sit anywhere on the bus but towards the front. They would make it clear to me that if they sat anywhere else on the bus, they would literally die within minutes. (Seriously—people tried to tell me this.)

Any such attempts I politely disregarded, and I explained to them that if this were truly the case, they probably shouldn't have come on this kind of a trip to begin with. (And they could probably use their doctor's note to get them an airline discount back to New York. As we were still at the airport, I even offered to escort them back to the ticket counter to begin the proceedings. In three years no one ever took me up on this.)

Still, at some point everyone would have to get off the bus. Not because we had arrived at where we were supposed to go, but because the bus would inevitably break down. Occasionally we somehow managed to get to a gas station or some other place where they could all at least get a soda or makes calls on a payphone. But just like it happens in the movies, more often than not we would break down by the side of the road, where we would be marooned until they could send us another bus.

Just waiting for a replacement bus could take up to five hours, because despite how frequently their buses broke down, the company didn't keep many spares on hand. (Remember, the name of the company was "Discount Travel.") As we were in the middle of the desert, the only shade provided was usually by the bus itself, so everyone would be leaning against it.

As the sun moved, everyone would gradually huddle closer together as the shaded area got smaller and smaller. Even at the time, I found the whole thing sort of comical, although of course I kept that to myself. I knew enough not to laugh at these people, particularly since I was in the identical situation. But I try to make a habit out of always finding humor in everything—*everything*!

During the times that the buses moved as they were intended to, we would stop at the various destinations on our route, usually for an hour or ninety minutes. I would try to tell everyone that it was *imperative* that we kept to our schedule, so would they *please* be back on the bus by a certain time. When that time rolled around, I would usually see that as few as half the people in the group actually came back, the others still meandering about, oblivious of what I had told them.

So I was quite literally begging and pleading with people just to do something that I probably shouldn't even need to ask them to do at all. And they disregarded it. But I figured out the reason that this was happening: because they knew perfectly well that the bus was never going to leave without them.

Thus starting with the next stop, I then tried a different approach (one that I am actually quite proud of thinking up). The revised announcement now went something like: "Ladies and gentlemen, we are now arriving at [wherever we were]. Now I know you're all going to love this place so much that some of you might want to stay longer than we have time for today. So if you're not back on the bus by noon, I'm going to assume that you want to stay a bit longer and let us leave without you. You can ask me now for the name of the hotel, and you can easily get there on your own using a taxi or public transportation. Enjoy!"

Lo and behold, *every last person* would be present and accounted for when it was time for the bus to leave (in most cases, even five to ten minutes early). Never underestimate the power of reverse psychology (or the cost of a taxi ride between two points in the middle of nowhere).

Another thing that sometimes took a bit of persuasion—if not manipulation—was the tips. The brochure had already made it abundantly clear that tipping me for the trip was expected. (And the tips, for me, weren't just gravy—I was paid a low wage for the job because gratuities were expected to make up the bulk of my overall income.)

The one thing I tried to avoid happening at all costs was the group thinking that they could collectively take care of the gratuity by passing a hat around and having everyone drop money in. This was absolutely not how I wanted to collect my tips. First of all, this wasn't some coffee shop in the East Village where I had just played folk songs on my acoustic guitar.

Yet at the beginning of one of my first trips, a self-proclaimed do-gooder named Paul, thinking that he was doing me a favor, took off his hat and began passing it around immediately after the bus started rolling. I called this "The Hat of Death."

You might be wondering what difference it made how I received the tips as long as the money was all green. Well, with the hat I'd end up getting less—considerably less. People were told up front that for my gratuity what was generally considered acceptable was ten to fifteen dollars (which wasn't really that much, even for people who could only spend four hundred dollars on a vacation package).

However, if they were to drop their money in a hat, I would have no way of knowing who contributed what, so everyone could feel that they satisfied their tip obligation even if they had put in less than ten dollars. In some cases we were talking about way less; occasionally someone would try to get away with a contribution of *fifty cents*. I knew I was screwed once I started hearing coins drop.

So I would be a bit more literal in the way that I would ask that people not pass around a hat. I would simply ask them: "Please don't pass around a hat." But then I'd pull another little mind-trip by telling them why "a personal 'thank you' would mean just as much to me as cash." I knew that this was going to get me appropriate tips, because nobody was about to stiff me to my face. (Well, almost nobody.)

I haven't even yet mentioned the hotels we'd be staying at. If during the bus trip people were hoping against hope that the accommodations would at least be an improvement over the method of transport, they were in for another disappointment.

Back in Los Angeles, we were usually put up at a hotel that was on the corner of Sunset Boulevard and Western Avenue. This happened to be the place where illegal immigrants would often stay after sneaking over the border while waiting for their "tour guide" to put them in the trunk of a Ford Focus for the next leg of their "trip." (Yet most of them were probably having a better time than we were.)

One time a member of my tour group opened the door to their hotel room to find a homeless man sleeping on the bed. Management kicked him out, but somehow they were reluctant to have the room made up again for their paying guest. The excuse was something along the lines of "he wasn't actually under the covers."

Did people complain? *You better believe it*. But I had yet another spiel for dealing with the imminent grievances regarding the hotel rooms (mainly because I wasn't actually in a position to do anything about it). Whenever people demanded to be immediately moved to a better hotel, I would take out a copy of the brochure (which I always kept handy).

I would pretend to study it closely for a couple of seconds before telling them that we would be happy to move them to a "better" hotel, as it was stated we would in the information they received prior to the tour. All they had to do was pay to be upgraded to a higher-tier vacation package. (Keep in mind, these were some of the people who wanted to tip me half a dollar). So almost without fail they would withdraw their complaint and say they decided to make the best of what they had gotten, and maybe even soak in the local ambience (which in this neighborhood was a polite term for "danger.")

One time we were at the end of the tour, in San Francisco. The hotel we had been booked in for this trip was another complete fleabag, possibly worse than the places the company usually booked (which even I didn't think was possible). For openers, the broom closet-sized elevator could only carry either a single person or two bags at a time, so it would take an hour just for everyone to even get to their rooms (and once they had gotten there, they wished they'd have had to wait longer).

But this is one trip that I will absolutely never forget. Not in a million years. I shall explain the reason.

I was at the "front desk" (which was actually a bridge table with a folding chair) counting the seconds until everyone would come to me and start complaining. I was all ready with my brochure "information." I also assumed I was prepared because by that point I must have heard every last type of gripe that anyone could come up with. However, the very first complaint I got on that day was one that I don't think anyone could've seen coming.

I felt a tug on my shirt and looked down. It was a very small, very fragile-looking lady about eighty-two years old. Through everything—the lousy bus rides through the hot deserts, the equally abysmal accommodations in Vegas and LA—she had not uttered a peep.

But she was about to make up for lost time, to say the least. Not by being loud or aggressive or even particularly assertive, but rather how she was about to analogize our situation.

"Bob," she said, in a heavy Eastern European accent, "I have to tell you something . . ."

She rolled up her sleeve to reveal a six-digit number tattooed on her arm in black ink. This woman had been held in a Nazi concentration camp.

Being Jewish, I'm particularly sensitive to the unspeakable tragedy of the Holocaust. But I couldn't understand why this woman had decided to pick this moment to reveal this about herself to me.

It turns out she was trying to illustrate a point, which she then explained. "Listen," she said. "I'm not a complainer, Bob. And I'm not looking for sympathy. I was in Auschwitz concentration camp. And I must tell you . . ." She took a big sigh before continuing: "My room there was better than the room they gave me here."

Needless to say, the brochure went right back into my pocket. There was clearly nothing I could say or do, other than to offer to give my own room to her (which I did and she accepted).

As inconceivable as this was, it wasn't the final straw. I had come out to LA just to work this job, and my plans to stick with it had not changed. But as much as these buses could never be relied upon even to simply move forward, my own professional life was about to take a 180-degree turn.

Chapter Three

Laverne & Shirley

Part I: Schlemiel

The story of how I broke into TV could have been something right out of a TV script—except that anyone watching would probably have said, "Oh, come on! That would *never* happen in real life!"

And yet it did. Without having ever worked a single day in television (or radio, or film), I was hired for the writing staff on the number one show on network television at the time. It was almost like walking in off the streets and getting to join The Beatles. (Sure, as Ringo, but nevertheless . . .)

Laverne & Shirley had premiered in early 1976 as a mid-season replacement show on ABC. The series revolved around a pair of young women who had previously been introduced on *Happy Days* as two of the many female acquaintances of ladies' man Fonzie, played by Henry Winkler.

My becoming involved with the show was particularly surreal considering where I was in my career—and my life—at that point. I was still living in Los Angeles and now several years into my thirties. The novelty of working as a West Coast bus tour guide was beginning to wear thin (and if you read the preceding chapter, hopefully you have an idea why).

I had decided that I would leave my current situation and move down to St. Martin in the Caribbean. There, a friend had offered me a job managing his bar in exchange for 25 percent ownership. It sounded like a pretty good deal, especially considering my dead-end tour guide situation.

I had been on the fence about it, because I did like LA.

Among the aspects of my life I was still enjoying was the improv comedy class that I had been involved with. The fact that Robin Williams was also a member (more on him later) suggests that there were a few serious-minded performers among us. I, however, had been doing the class purely for fun, not expecting or even necessarily wanting to be "discovered."

Another performer I knew from the group at the time was a guy named Marc Sotkin. One afternoon I happened to be playing a game of paddle tennis with him in Venice Beach. I told him (between serves) about the dissatisfaction I was feeling with my current employment as a tour guide and my tentative plans to leave town. He suggested that I hold off on making any final decisions, backing up the advice by saying only, "Something might happen. And soon."

I already knew that Sotkin had been working as a staff writer on *Laverne & Shirley*. However, at the time he was also on the cusp of being promoted to producer. He didn't mention this during our game, let alone that it could have an effect on me. Nonetheless, I took his advice and held off on packing my bags for the islands.

A couple of weeks later, he revealed to me the reason he had told me to give LA one more chance. His promotion to producer went through, and as he was now in a position to hire people, he wanted to know if I might be in interested becoming part of the show's writing staff.

I was both surprised and elated, and needless to say I accepted the offer without a moment's hesitation. I couldn't believe my luck: just weeks earlier I had been trying to keep ninety bus tourists from rioting over being booked at run-down hotels, and now I was about to become a writer on the highest-rated show in television. (If he had offered me just about any job on the show—even just gofer—I would have taken it.)

Sotkin figured I would make a good sitcom writer from what he saw during my improv performances. He felt my sense of humor was in sync with what they were looking for on the show. His instinct is what would lead me on this life-changing path.

He was right at least in the assumption that I had a writer's imagination, since it was already getting carried away with me a bit. This is how I honestly visualized my first day working on *Laverne & Shirley*: I would drive up to the studio where a friendly, Norman Rockwell-esque security guard named "Jimmy" would address me as "Mr. P." and raise the gate for me before giving me a two-finger salute and telling me to have a nice day. And then I would drive up to my very own parking space (with my name on it, of course) right next to my office (yes, I had an office) and be on the way to my effortless conquest of the TV sitcom world.

That first day arriving at the studio instead turned into Phase One in my rude awakening. When I actually got there, the guard's name wasn't Jimmy, a fact unaltered by my attempt to address him as such. After I identified myself, he checked his clipboard and (eventually) found my name, which was quite literally at the bottom of the list. When I asked where my parking spot was, he looked at me as if I were crazy—crazy even for Los Angeles, which is saying something.

He gave me directions to where it was okay for me to park, which ultimately meant driving so far I thought I was going to wind up back in Rhode Island. I finally ended up eight blocks away next to a dumpster behind a Mexican restaurant. The only words on it were not my name but rather *Prohibido Holgazaner* ("No Loitering").

After the eight-block walk back, I at long last got inside the studio, and I was taken to the writer's room to meet the staff I had agreed to join. Sotkin introduced me and told them all how amazingly funny he thought I was. I know he was just trying to help (he hired me, after all), but already I knew that he had inadvertently oversold me.

Accordingly, I was greeted mostly with indifferent grunts by my new colleagues. So any preconceived notions I may have had about the comedy writing staff as a merry bunch of lads laughing heartily, throwing water balloons, and playfully zapping each other with joy buzzers was dispelled quickly after mere minutes of exposure to the group. These guys were funny but also noticeably bitter, which I would later find out was fairly typical of sitcom writers.

I realize I'm not the first person to make the assessment, but pretty much on that first day I found it to be very true that comedy writers are, by and large, not happy people. Most of them had been victims of bullying and ostracizing as children, the kind that causes one to go very far inside oneself emotionally until they arrive at the level of introspection that is often (or even usually) necessary for being able to craft humor.

Having had no experience as a writer—let alone a member of a writing *staff*—I didn't immediately fit in. Logically, my comfort level should've been increasing the longer I was there, but during my difficult first few weeks I found it actually moving in the opposite direction. At every meeting, I would become less willing—or able—to chime in vocally than I had been at the previous one, and that rabbit hole kept getting deeper.

Ever since I first sat down, I had had a terrible feeling that the build-up Sotkin had given me upon my introduction (well-meaning though it may have been) was going to come back to bite me. I was now amusing these guys all right, but quite unintentionally and for all the wrong reasons. I could tell they were actually starting to get off on watching me struggling to keep up.

This basically came to a head when another producer, Chris Thompson, gave me a "gift": a t-shirt that read "I'LL BE FUNNY SOON." I realize this doesn't sound like anything more serious than some good-natured ribbing between coworkers. But trust me when I say that I was fully aware of it being a very real and calculated swipe at me. I knew at that moment I was every bit as screwed as Fredo Corleone after getting the "kiss of death" from his brother Michael in *The Godfather Part II*.

Still, I had committed to this and I was determined to make it work. I didn't feel like spending the rest of my life telling war stories about how I was handed the opportunity of a lifetime only to have the television industry chew me up and spit me out.

If the writing staff was something of a surprise, some members of the cast weren't exactly what I had been expecting either. By now most people are aware of the somewhat volatile relationship between the show's two stars, Penny Marshall (Laverne) and Cindy Williams (Shirley). Marshall was the sister of series creator/producer Garry Marshall, and their sister and father also worked on the show. From the very beginning, Williams had always felt as though the deck was stacked against her, which in turn caused a great deal of tension.

The antagonism between the two lead actresses has commonly been illustrated by the story about how both of them would count the lines in the script in order to make sure

Bob with stars Penny Marshall (left) and Cindy Williams (right)

the other wasn't getting more attention or jokes. This was done quite openly, often with both of them sitting at the same table where the entire cast would do the reading every week.

For anyone who might not know, a "table-read" is standard practice not just on sitcoms but all TV shows and theater productions (and even feature films). Once the script is complete, all the actors (out of costume) will sit at a table holding the script and everyone reads their lines. This is done so that everyone gets to "hear" the dialogue and get a sense of how good it is (or isn't). When I first saw Marshall and Williams counting the lines I found it a bit unnerving, although I would later find out that this actually happens fairly often elsewhere.

Despite any personal differences they might have had, the actors would tend to form a united front against the writers. David L. Lander, who played Squiggy on the show, had a favorite routine he occasionally used for expressing dissatisfaction with what we'd written: He would hold a copy of the week's script, pretend to sniff it, and say, "Hey, does anyone else smell this? It's kind of familiar. Oh yeah, it smells like *crap*!" before throwing it in the nearest trash bin (which for us meant a long night of rewriting).

Part II: Schlimazel

One afternoon, after I had been there for about three months, Garry Marshall approached me just as a taping was about to get underway. Marshall, at least when I worked with him, was always a man of few words. This came out as a kind of shorthand that, oddly enough, we all understood.

Still, that day he said five words to me that would be enough to alter the course of my entire life: "Bob. Audience. Go. *Be funny*."

He was telling me to go do the audience warmup. (See? Even *you* understand the short-hand now.)

Laverne & Shirley generally took about three hours to tape an episode, which was pretty much standard back then. But also as on most other shows, audience warmup was thought of as—at best—only a minor part of the proceedings, probably at about the same level as making sure the pitchers of ice water backstage stayed filled.

Hiring an outsider just to do audience warmup was something that was usually never even considered at the time. When *Laverne & Shirley* first came on, it was being handled by Fred Fox Jr., a writer for *Happy Days* who was also doing the warmup for that show (which filmed at the stage next door).

As soon as Fox decided he didn't want to do both shows, warmup on *Laverne* basically fell to any member of the writing staff chosen at random (which as I understand it was the case on most sitcoms), who in turn would be thrown an extra fifty dollars for their trouble. Most of the other writers grumbled at being assigned this extra bit of work, even with the life-altering fifty bucks. But all and all, the undertaking was still seen as such an afterthought that in a pinch they probably would've just told the janitor to go do it.

But as soon as I got up there on Marshall's command, the energy that I projected and the (sincere) enthusiasm which I clearly had for being there were obvious. And the audience reacted accordingly. The episode wrapped, and within minutes Marshall asked me if I wanted to do warmup at every taping for the rest of the season—which evolved into doing the rest of the show's run.

Throughout my career, one of the most common questions I've been asked is, "Are you ever nervous when you go out there among the audience?" Honestly, I wasn't even nervous that first time. Having been working as a tour guide for years, I was very much used to getting up in front of a crowd of strangers and having to keep them not just occupied but— as much as possible—*happy* while they were waiting for something else to happen.

Still, only about ten episodes into doing the warmup, we had a situation with the studio audience so absurd that it could've been something right out of the show. With the audience in place, the cast began doing the scenes. And *nobody* was laughing. Not a single person.

The actors were clearly dumbfounded as the technicians scrambled to figure out if there was some problem that was preventing the audience from hearing the dialogue. They found none. The script had seemed okay at the table read and everything appeared fine at rehearsal. What could possibly be going on?

I got the answer after being approached by an Asian man wearing a suit whom I had never seen before. It seemed that the entire audience for that week's show consisted of a tour group from Taiwan, none of whom understood English. (The reason I had not noticed this irregularity was that I would start the warmup from the stage, where the spotlight would be on me and there'd be no light on the audience.)

We considered rescheduling the taping, but that would have meant paying everyone extra. Plus, these people were guests not only at our show but in our country, and we didn't want to insult them.

Thus, the show went on. The actors did all the scenes to more maddening silence. Then we gave the man, who was their translator, a copy of the script. He stood in the middle of the bleachers and read all the lines out loud in Chinese.

Now, the crowd (finally) laughed hysterically. We were happy to discover that our show's humor quite literally translated. But nonetheless, it was all very surreal. And needless to say, when the episode aired we used a laugh track.

As much as I had clearly found my niche, I wasn't about to give up my position on the writing staff. Warmup was still only paying the fifty bucks a week, so that would have been a considerable drop in salary.

At the same time, despite my shaky start I was finally gaining confidence as a writer. On May 6, 1980, *Laverne & Shirley* aired the first episode that I was ever screen-credited for. It was called "The Diner," and the approach was as rudimentary as the title: simply the time-tested comedic idea that anything that can go wrong will go wrong, as the two main characters worked at a diner (or tried to) during the lunch rush.

Bob (standing, second from right) with the writing staff of Laverne & Shirley *and Garry Marshall (seated on ground)*

In 1999, *TV Guide* would do a cover story on the fifty funniest TV moments of all time, and "The Diner"—written by me, Bob Perlow, the one-time black sheep of the writing staff—was the only episode of *Laverne & Shirley* to make the list. The magazine called it "one of the funniest bits of physical comedy since Lucy and Ethel went to work in a candy factory." *Did I mention I wrote it?*

As well as that episode turned out (and I think I felt it even at the time), I concluded that I wasn't comfortable writing on my own. I decided to contact another comedy writer I knew: Gene Braunstein, whom I would always call "Geno." (And I still do.) He and I had met a decade earlier through a mutual friend, who just happened to be Jay Leno. (Much more about him later, I promise!)

Jay had been roommates with both Geno and me on different occasions (Geno in college, then me later on in LA). At the time I was writing on *Laverne & Shirley*, both of them were writing for *Good Times* star Jimmy "J. J." Walker's

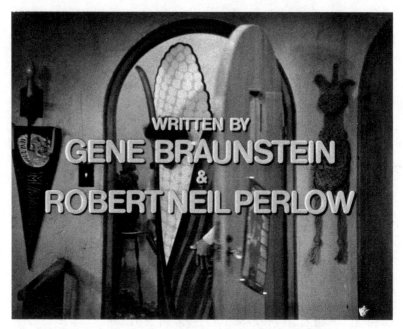

Credits from an episode written by Bob and Gene Braunstein

stand-up act, while Geno was also making ends meet with a job in a local tobacco shop.

Geno would become my permanent writing partner, and together we penned scripts for sitcoms over the next twenty years. Unfortunately, the first episode we coscripted for *Laverne & Shirley* wasn't going to make any all-time-funniest lists: it was part one of a two-part episode in which Laverne ends up on death row awaiting execution. It was about as plausible—and funny—as it sounds.

Part III: Hasenpfeffer Incorporated

By that point, the show itself had been on the TV equivalent of death row for a while. The trouble had started several seasons earlier. Tuesday nights at 8:30, *Laverne* had been number one or close to it since debuting. Despite this, the network decided to move the show out of that timeslot in the fall of 1979. The ratings plummeted.

Hence, we came into the sixth season rating-challenged for the first time. All of us knew that meant making a major change in the show, one that would recapture the viewer's attention (if nothing else). This, in turn, we realized inevitably meant either adding a small child to the cast or changing the show's locale.

It was decided on the latter: Laverne and Shirley would move from Milwaukee to Los Angeles. All the supporting characters would be following them, for some reason. (*Oh wait*, I know the reason: they had *contracts* and would have to get paid whether they "moved" or not. So they moved.)

In the twenty-first century, this would come to be known as "jumping the shark." The term, which identifies the moment or event on a show when it becomes clear that they've crossed over into the realm of "just pushing it," comes from a 1977 episode of parent series *Happy Days* in which the Fonz literally jumps (on water skis) over a shark.

That isn't to say that the California-based seasons of *Laverne* didn't produce its share of decent episodes. Two new cast members were introduced, including a former Heisman trophy winner with movie star looks, Ed Marinaro (who had appeared in season five in a different role), and Leslie Easterbrook, who played a character named Rhonda.

Although both newcomers would fit into the cast nicely, we didn't need a hip term like "jump the shark" to realize that the show's best years were behind it. All the joy, fun, and energy that once defined putting the show together week after week was no longer evident among either the actors or the writers. It was like being employed at a company that everyone knew was on the verge of going under.

Cindy Williams left the show at the beginning of what would ultimately be the final season. Shirley stayed in the title but otherwise took what little was left of the show's enthusiasm with her. It's a bit ironic that a show about factory workers trying to rise above their situation ("make their dreams come true," as the theme song reminded us) would end with the people creating it just punching the clock indifferently.

Bob with Cindy Williams, who played Shirley Feeney

The previous year *M*A*S*H* had aired its final episode, which became the most-watched TV program of all time. (The record still stands.) Doing a "final episode" of *Laverne & Shirley* would have been logical, good for the ratings, and, frankly, respectful: maybe having Laverne get married, or bringing Shirley back for one last appearance. But we couldn't even be bothered—that's the level of apathy we had reached. The very last scene of the series ended up being Carmine (Eddie Mekka) singing "Aquarius" from the musical *Hair*. But otherwise the show ended on a low note.

Three decades later, I don't think anyone is certain just how we ended up on *Hair*. But the first two lines of the song

("When the moon is in the seventh house/And Jupiter aligns with Mars") do sort of describe what had happened to me. My friendship with Sotkin, Marshall telling me to warm up the audience when he did, and my varying backgrounds as a tour guide, a teacher, and an improv comic had all synced to form what would become my not only successful but also very unique and rewarding future.

Sure, everyone who had at one time or another been involved with the show could now put their contribution to a big hit TV series on their résumé. However, coming out of my own five years on *Laverne & Shirley*, I hadn't merely launched a career.

I had *invented* one.

Chapter Four

Angie

Angie is not a particularly well-remembered show, but there might not be any that's more important in terms of my own career. This is the sitcom on which I solidified the general method of doing audience warmup, which I would continue for the next thirty-five years.

I was also hoping to establish the idea of someone being hired from outside the show to focus on the audience warmup and do nothing else. This was actually *not* unprecedented, although it was certainly unusual: I guesstimate that maybe 2 percent of all sitcom tapings were being done by someone who had no other function on the show (usually a stand-up comic).

After doing the warmup for a single episode of *Laverne & Shirley* immediately turned into doing it week-in and week-out, I realized I had tapped into something. But also I knew the show wasn't going to last forever. (It only seemed to, if you watched any of the final season, especially the "death row" episode . . . and I *wrote* that one.)

One thing I did not want to do was go back to being a tour guide. My experience on *Laverne* probably qualified me to go work as a staff writer on another sitcom, but the problem was that there would be dozens or even hundreds of other writers equally—or more—qualified going out for the same positions. Landing another writing job wasn't going to be a question of how "big" the show was; it would be experience, which most of those writers would have more of than I did.

But with audience warmup, I had stumbled onto something not only that I was capable of doing, but for which at the moment there was pretty much no competition. Nobody (or almost nobody) else had thought to pursue it as its own thing. The trick now was convincing others—that is, the ones in a positon to pay—that it could in fact be a full-time career.

So what I needed to find now was another sitcom, probably a smaller show (in terms of ratings), that I could use as both my testing ground and my demonstration model to advertise my abilities to other sitcom producers who might be willing to hire me.

Angie first came on the air as a mid-season replacement in February 1979. The show's star, Donna Pescow, had appeared in the movie *Saturday Night Fever*, the quintessential depiction of the oversexed disco era. The sitcom, thematically, would be the virtual antithesis, demonstrating old-fashioned traditional romance to a generation that seemed to have forgotten such a thing existed.

The show was a sort of modern Cinderella story about a girl from a working-class background who marries a rich, handsome young doctor. This being post-woman's movement, however, she holds on to a degree of the independence that she had before they met (i.e., she continues to work the same waitressing job).

Today *Angie* is probably only noteworthy to most of the public for two of its other cast members. The show's male lead, Robert Hayes, starred in the classic comedy film *Airplane!* and would retain some visibility throughout the Eighties; Doris Roberts played the Italian American mother-in-law, a very similar role to that which she would later have for nine seasons on *Everybody Loves Raymond*.

Angie was being filmed on the Paramount lot where I had already been working, and it was even cocreated by Garry Marshall. (So I guess I didn't wander that far from home after all.) I approached the show's producers, identifying myself as a writer from *Laverne & Shirley*, and told them that I was there to do audience warmup for them.

They were naturally confused. They were pretty sure they hadn't sent for me, and I wasn't a writer—or anything else— on their show. But I told them to trust me. The conversation then turned, as it inevitably does in show business, to money. When they asked me how much I would want to be paid for what I was offering to do, I braced myself and got my nerve up before asking for the ungodly sum of three hundred dollars.

From the look I got, you'd think I had been asking for their firstborn. They told me absolutely not. They already had one of their own staff writers to do it for fifty bucks, so why would they need someone from the outside to handle it, let alone at six times the money?

I didn't even bother trying to get them to meet me halfway. Rather, I met them *no* part of the way: I said I would do it for free.

I realize this hardly sounds like particularly shrewd negotiating on my part, especially considering that I have a master's degree in business (albeit from the University of Rhode Island). In fact, when all was said and done, I wasn't even going to break even; I would be doing this at a loss. No, I'm not talking about gas money. Rather, part of my plan involved literally *buying* the cooperation of the *Angie* studio audience.

One thing that the general public can never get enough of—as I learned from my years as a tour guide—is, oddly enough, t-shirts. I've seen people, even those of means, quite literally fight over them. This is why t-shirts have always been the go-to souvenir for just about every public event, from church picnics to heavy metal concerts to, yes, discount travel destinations. Ordinary people are usually all too happy to pony up cold hard cash for them, but if the t-shirts just happen to be free, all the better.

In this case I wouldn't be giving out shirts with the name of the show or the ABC logo or anything else directly connected to the event on them. That's because the show didn't have any merchandise made up yet, and I certainly wasn't about to pay for that out of my pocket. I still wanted to utilize this general idea but had a somewhat more economical strategy, as I knew that pretty much any t-shirts would probably do the trick (if only because nobody was going to be going to a sitcom taping expecting shirts at all).

It ended up being *just* a bit more complicated than I imagined. I had assumed that at the very least I knew where to buy the shirts, figuring I would simply go down to the boardwalk on Venice Beach where all the souvenir shops were.

When I got to Venice Beach I was surprised to find that the area had undergone a major changeover, and most of the souvenir stores were now owned and operated by foreigners. To keep this inoffensive, I won't specify what region these foreigners were from; we'll just say they weren't American and leave it at that.

Please don't get me wrong: I believe everyone in our country has the right to practice free enterprise. But people from different cultures often have their own way of doing things, and this created something of an obstacle for me.

Almost all of these stores were advertising t-shirts at a cost of "3 for $10." I guess that's probably a bargain if three are all you actually want. But I was looking to buy several hundred. I asked at every single store if they could offer me a price break for buying in bulk.

Not one did. I stared to wonder if "3 for $10" were the only words any of these guys actually knew in English, because those were pretty much the only words I heard any of them say. Thankfully, towards the end of the boardwalk, I came across a store run by two savvy guys named Alan and Fred. They were all too happy to cut me "such a deal" on several hundred shirts.

None of these shirts were anything particularly fancy: most of them just said either "CALIFORNIA" or "VENICE BEACH" on them. But I only needed t-shirts with some design or writing on them, so these could have said "I KILL BUNNIES" for all it mattered.

Either way, I was now fully armed with my weapon of choice (the t-shirts) and I approached going to do warmup for *Angie* as if I was heading into battle. I was actually only planning to give about ten away during the taping (which ultimately turned into about fifty); but I wanted to keep an ample supply on hand, since I guessed—correctly—that I'd be giving away a lot of t-shirts in the foreseeable future and these would keep.

One practice that had previously been common at sitcom tapings was giving candy bars out to the audience members (which Garry Marshall would do on *Happy Days*). There were two basic problems with that idea: First of all, the crinkling noise being made by the wrappers would get picked up by the microphones and throw the audio off. Second, the audience would get a sugar rush and be attentive and energetic, but then this would be followed by the inevitable crash, which made their reactions to the show inconsistent.

Hence, t-shirts are a far better idea, and I wasn't even shy about taking credit for it. In 1998 I was interviewed for a *New York Times* article about live sitcom audiences where I told them, "I think I invented t-shirts." A couple of years later Al Gore would get in some trouble for supposedly claiming he invented the Internet, so I think I should probably clarify my statement.

Actually what I invented was the idea of giving them away to sitcom studio audiences, because this is also something that no one else had done before. For years people would ask me, "Isn't that, like, a bribe?" I would always respond, "Don't be ridiculous. It isn't *like* a bribe. It *is* a bribe."

Sure, giveaways were already common at, say, sporting events, but those happen all over the country. No one had thought to give away souvenirs to a sitcom audience, and my educated guess is that they simply assumed that the crowd of mostly tourists would be dazzled enough by just the chance to watch a TV show being filmed. They may not have been *wrong* necessarily, but what I was doing was taking it up a notch.

The t-shirts, as I predicted, were a hit. But probably the most important thing I did at the taping came at the end, after everything had been filmed and, at least in theory, the studio audience served no additional purpose to the show. What

I did was make certain that the audience gave a standing ovation, not just to the actors but to everyone who worked on the show, starting with the crew and most importantly the writers and producers.

And I didn't simply say, "Please give a standing ovation." First for the crew, then for the writers, then finally the actors, I would (out of the line of sight of the producers) give the audience the "stand up" gesture and keep doing it until every last audience member rose to their feet. When the producers got their ovation, I don't mind saying that with their egos, they naturally thought it was all happening on the spur of the moment.

I didn't stop there. I went as far as to bring in music specifically for this, which would provide a whole soundtrack for the standing ovations. (Wow, I clearly put a lot of planning into something that is supposed to be spontaneous.) I brought the tunes in on eight-track cartridges. (Don't feel bad if you're too young to remember those. I feel bad that I'm old enough to have used them.)

I would utilize the help of the show's sound guys, which is something else I would end up doing pretty much for the rest of my career, whether it was for something like this or for a skit of some kind. Almost all of the time, they were happy to help me—they thought that it was fun being part of what I was doing, something that was different, more immediate, and a bit more creative than their usual technical responsibilities.

What I was hoping to do here was have the music convey a mood of victory. This is what I wanted the audience to feel they had just witnessed, to have them recognize that it was the crew, writers, and cast who were the ones responsible. So I would use the Olympic fanfare, or "Pomp and Circumstance" (which most people know as "The Graduation Song") or even "America the Beautiful." Anything that sounded grandiose.

The music choice for when the actors came out on stage was a bit more obvious: the show's theme song, "Different Worlds." Needless to say, I didn't need to bring this one in with me—the sound guys already had it. The song was performed by Maureen McGovern, who was best known for singing the themes to the era-defining early Seventies disaster movies *The Poseidon Adventure* and *The Towering Inferno*.

The connection between those two films and the end of the *Angie* taping may not have been a complete non-sequitur: with the music and standing ovations, I was trying to transform the last few minutes of the taping of this sweet little sitcom into a full-on *epic*. If there had been a safe way to set off fireworks indoors, I probably would've done that.

By the way, I honestly was never just playing on the egos of the people who worked on the show; I sincerely believed that the standing ovation was something they'd all earned. Then again, one thing that the producers never found out is that I gave t-shirts out as rewards to the audience members whom I decided were the "best," because they laughed the most or gave the most enthusiastic cheers. (Look, I admitted the shirts were a bribe, didn't I?)

That was pretty much it as far as this taping went. I hadn't yet created any of the stunts or audience participation activities that I would do later (and that I'll be describing in future chapters). Those would have to evolve over the next thirty-five years.

For now, however, what I had done was enough. Once this taping of *Angie* wrapped, the response I got from the producers was as immediate as it had been on *Laverne & Shirley*: what they had just witnessed was like nothing they had ever seen in terms of audience warmup.

Most importantly, they realized just how beneficial it potentially was to what they were doing: a more enthusiastic audience means "happier" actors, which means better performances, which means a better show. Maintaining a high level of morale for the behind-the-scenes team was important for the same reasons.

The producers asked me to come back to do all future tapings and now gladly agreed to my outrageous three-hundred-dollars-a-show fee. They drew the line at offering more, but they did reimburse me for the t-shirts from that taping and all future ones.

It's not for me to say whether I would eventually become the best warmup person in the business. However, I think it's safe for me to take credit for innovating it on the level that I did.

And this, as they say, was only the beginning (though no one is ever able to explain who "they" are).

Chapter Five

Mork & Mindy

The first time I ever encountered Robin Williams, he was watching me perform. Yes, you read that correctly—he was watching me. It was 1976, and we were both participants in the Los Angeles improv comedy workshop Off the Wall.

It was my turn to get up and improvise a scene, and Williams, who would have been about twenty-five years old at the time, was sitting in the audience. When I was done, I saw him—and we hadn't even been officially introduced yet—give me a "thumbs up" and an approving grin. This was my first time ever getting up to improvise a scene, so you tend to remember a gesture like that, no matter who it's from.

A short time later, it was his turn to go up onstage and perform. After he was done, I couldn't bring myself to return the positive gesture of approval that he had given me before. It wasn't because I didn't think he was any good. Quite the contrary: I thought that Williams was so brilliant while he was up there that I was rendered speechless by what I had just watched. I could see from that brief scene that he was really something outstanding.

One thing about Williams that was already obvious to me by then was the fact that he was "always on"—he would be spontaneously doing impressions and riffing 24/7. Whenever a celebrity has a very distinct public persona, the question always becomes, "Is it an act?" In the case of Robin Williams, it was an act, but it was one that in public at least he would never shut off—possibly because he couldn't, but also possibly because he didn't want to.

Although not that much time would have passed by the

next time I saw Robin Williams, it was enough for him to emerge as a bona fide superstar. This was when I would begin doing warmup for his show *Mork & Mindy*, which was the second big hit I did after *Laverne & Shirley*.

Both shows were produced by Garry Marshall and spun off from *Happy Days*. The simple plot of *Mork & Mindy* involved Williams playing an alien from the planet Ork who comes to Earth to observe humans and our civilization while being helped by an Earth girl, who was played by Pam Dawber.

Mork is where the world would get its first extended look at his talents, the mile-a-minute energy that included quips, mime-based physical gestures, and an infinity of character voices, all balanced by precision comedic timing. For as much as the world had never seen a performer like him, Robin Williams may as well have been an alien in real life.

Besides Williams, the other legacy of the show sadly lies in its notoriety—or perhaps infamy—for making completely unnecessary sweeping changes (mostly in terms of the hiring and firing of supporting cast members) throughout its run, starting at the beginning of season two.

This was also when I began on *Mork*, after the ratings had already plummeted and reviewers were vehemently expressing just-kill-me-now disappointment with the changes. So I'm certain a lot of people familiar with the show's history are probably right now thinking, "Aw, Bob, you missed the good year!"

On paper, maybe, but three years of working with Robin Williams in a live setting would always keep anyone on their toes, to put it mildly. If you only watched the show at home, you got just a taste of what was actually going on.

I've already described the overall low mood that could be felt on the set of *Laverne & Shirley* once it became clear that the show was on borrowed time, even before it was formally cancelled. By contrast, even though *Mork* would be plagued by all-too-conspicuous problems for about three-quarters of its run, Williams refused to let the party end or even slow down.

Bob with Robin Williams

If you came to a taping of *Mork & Mindy,* no matter how good (or bad) the episode you would later see at home was, you would invariably be treated to a whole other show courtesy of Robin Williams. Between every scene, Williams would go right out into the crowd and simply be brilliantly funny off-the-cuff: anything about an audience member— what they looked like, what they were wearing, a common item they were holding—would become a springboard for an on-the-spot routine. Needless to say, the crowd loved it.

On stage and with cameras rolling, it wasn't much easier to predict what Williams might do next at any given time. Very few scenes he was in ended up being played verbatim as written in the script. Most sitcoms I've worked on do at least two full takes of every scene anyway, usually just to have some choice of what to use in the final edit. In most instances, however, the multiple takes are pretty much interchangeable.

This was not the case with *Mork*: Williams would ad lib incessantly, and never the same way twice. Although everything shot would follow the same basic storyline, the producers would end up with an embarrassment of riches with two or even three takes of the same scene. Each was probably about 50-75 percent different, but all equally brilliant.

This was my first year doing audience warmup full time, and I was still developing many of the regular audience-participation methods that I would use over the next thirty years. These included giveaways, dance contests, sing-alongs, and lots of audience interaction. But on Mork, I would never attempt to do any sort of my own comedy for the crowd. I knew enough to say, as the old vaudeville adage went, "I'm not following *that* act." I realized that after Robin Williams, anything I could come up with would probably seem about as funny as a monologue from *Death of a Salesman*. So I would stick to mostly just praising Williams (as well as giving away countless t-shirts).

Despite how much energy he was clearly burning through on the show, Williams hardly went straight home to his bathrobe, slippers, and herbal tea once *Mork* wrapped for the night. Rather, he spent most evenings performing either in local comedy clubs or right back at our old stomping ground, Off the Wall. He rarely made any extra money doing this; he was, quite simply, addicted to performing for an audience. It didn't really matter whether it was an audience of one or an audience of hundreds, just as long as he was onstage (and more importantly, to him, just "on").

On the unfortunate subject of addictions, anyone familiar

with Williams' history is probably assuming by now that cocaine use must have been playing a major role. All I can say about that is that I never noticed it in particular (although this being the era and environment that it was, even a worse-than-average level of cocaine abuse would not really have stood out).

Williams, on the other hand, would inevitably stand out no matter who else happened to be performing alongside him. While at various points there might have been as many as half a dozen regular supporting characters, it should have been obvious that trying to turn *Mork & Mindy* into an ensemble piece was frankly a waste of resources. The comedic presence of Robin Williams was honestly so overpowering that anyone who tried to share the stage with him might as well have been invisible.

I discovered this firsthand during our Off the Wall days when I had done several improv sessions with him—or tried to. But if you want to go a little further up the comedy ladder, you need only watch the annual *Comic Relief* specials from the Eighties, where basically the same thing happened even when Williams performed alongside genuinely gifted performers like the great Billy Crystal and Whoopi Goldberg. Anyone working in even marginally close proximity to Williams would pretty much evaporate. He was that good.

Back on *Mork*, this would usually even include Pam Dawber. Despite the character's name being in the show's title, and later efforts to follow her as she pursued a career in journalism (including an episode where she was assigned to interview Robin Williams), at the end of the day Mindy was mostly there only for Mork to play off.

Some say that Dawber was a saint for essentially volunteering to be a prop; others might suggest that second billing on a hit TV show is hardly a position to be pitied under any circumstances (even though the egos of most successful actors might disagree). Either way, Dawber always seemed relatively content with where she was. Plus she was always as sweet off stage as she was on.

Though ratings continued to slide, ABC renewed *Mork* for a fourth season in 1981, most likely because they would've lost more money if they didn't end up with enough episodes to create a syndication package. With one last chance to save the show, and recognizing a clear-cut make-or-break situation, producers decided to bring out "the big guns," which materialized in the form of comedy legend Jonathan Winters.

Bob with Pam Dawber

Winters had actually appeared on the show in the third season in a different role, but getting him on the show as a regular offered seemingly unlimited possibilities. Winters was more than just a successful veteran comic: many consider him to have invented modern improvisational comedy (at least in the form that it's generally practiced today), which was not simply Williams' professional stepping stone but also gave him license to be who he truly was as a performer. (Williams often described Winters as his idol.) Pairing the two in a weekly series seemed like an opportunity to make TV history.

I too was excited about the prospect of working with Jonathan Winters, and what it might mean to the show. However, during my first encounter with him (I really can't even call it a "meeting"), I ended up getting a bit more than I bargained for.

I was in the studio around the time the cast had just finished rehearsals for the afternoon. I walked onto the stage area, and there were two other people in the vicinity: One was the studio janitor, who was sweeping the floor, getting the stage ready for that night's taping. The second was none other than Jonathan Winters himself.

Only a couple of years into my own television career at the time, I was still prone to being starstruck as much as anyone else. Not to mention that being an improv comic, this was almost like a minor league baseball player getting to meet Babe Ruth (whom Winters actually resembled).

I said to the janitor, "That's Jonathan Winters!" as though uttering it out loud to another person would solidify the reality, even though I didn't expect the janitor to be surprised by the revelation.

This is when things began to take an odd turn. In reaction to what I had just said, the janitor began slowly walking— actually *sneaking*—away. Naturally, I was confused. You would think that someone who worked in a TV studio, even as a custodian, would be more or less indifferent to celebrity and would pretty much just say to me with a shrug, "Yeah, that's nice."

So why did this guy seem anxious, even desperate, to avoid Jonathan Winters? I wondered if maybe they had had a bad encounter earlier.

"Don't let him see you!" the janitor then warned me in a concerned whisper as he continued to back away.

Don't let him see *me*? I hadn't even *met* Winters yet. This was making less and less sense.

Being told to leave a particular celebrity alone is not unusual, as many of them simply do not want to be approached by strangers and doing so will result in them either ignoring you or even angrily demanding to know what you could possibly imagine gives you the right to waste their time. So I thought that was one of *those* warnings.

Not even close. Actually just the opposite, as I was about to find out. Essentially martyring himself to illustrate just what he had been trying to convey to me, the janitor reluctantly made eye contact with Winters. For just a moment, but that was all it took.

The legendary comedian immediately ran over to us and grabbed the broom away from the janitor, before breaking into the spontaneous character of a demanding army drill sergeant.

"*That's* no way to hold a rifle, *soldier!*" Winters barked out at the janitor playfully. Within minutes the comedian was also using the broom to mime pushing gunpowder into a cannon and then as a telescope, with corresponding new characters for each action.

The hapless janitor played along (he probably realized he didn't have a choice), taking the role of the solider. But all the while was giving me a "see what I mean?" look. He really only wanted to get his broom back so he could use it as, well, a *broom* and get back to his sweeping.

But I got his point: if you're going to approach Jonathan Winters or even catch his eye, you'd better have the time and patience to contend with twenty minutes or a half-hour of unrequested, though brilliant, spontaneous comedy.

Throughout that season, I found out more and more just

Bob with Jonathan Winters

how much it truly was impossible to have a casual or brief conversation with Jonathan Winters. You couldn't simply ask him, "How about this weather we're having?" or "Did you see the game last night?" and expect a straight answer. Like Williams, Winters was very much "always on."

What made Winters who he was, as a person and a performer, went a bit deeper than the standard "behind every comedian is a sad man" axiom. About twenty years earlier he had been institutionalized for about eight months on two separate occasions. Throughout his life Winters suffered from bipolar disorder, was susceptible to nervous breakdowns, and acknowledged that he would "hear voices."

It's not difficult to see why Williams not only idolized Winters but also probably felt deep empathy with him. The two appeared together on *Late Night with David Letterman* a few years after *Mork* finished. As Williams explained, "A man named Nielsen just said, 'Bag 'em both!'" Williams at one point affectionately called Winters "Dad," which instantly became a spontaneous four-minute father/son sketch. The two may not have been actually related, but the connection between them was just as strong as any actual blood bond I've ever seen.

Williams' already tireless energy and spontaneity in front of the *Mork* studio audience multiplied exponentially after he was joined by Winters, as both of them were now finally working with a genuine peer. Indeed, Winters may have been the only other performer—ever—whose performance Williams couldn't instantly reduce to an afterthought with his own. Since there were now two of them, my warmup contributions were fading even further into the background, but I was fine with that.

The director would yell "Cut!" at the end of a scene, which everyone else knows means "stop"; but to Williams and Winters—now free from the hindrance of the written word in the form of the actual script, which they often used only as a general guideline anyway—it became their cue to break into a usually brilliant, improvised, twenty-minute comedy routine. This happened three or four times at every taping.

In fact, it probably would have been a better idea to film and air those instead of what they ended up with. The fourth season began with Mork and Mindy getting married (itself probably an interesting—though obvious—enough twist to get some mileage out of), but a few episodes later, Mork literally lays an egg. The egg grows enormous until their "son," played by Winters, hatches out of it.

If adding a small child to a sitcom is generally seen as jumping the shark, then what must adding a *big* child be? Jumping a blue whale? Furthermore, the character Mearth (Mork:Ork, Mearth:Earth) was for the most part a routine child-in-a-man's-body gag that probably could have been played by any actor of the same approximate age and physical type. So home viewers, sadly, very seldom got to witness the full potential of the pairing of Robin Williams and Jonathan Winters. This would be the final season of *Mork and Mindy*.

In 2013 Jonathan Winters died at age eighty-seven, not long after losing his wife of nearly sixty years. Williams' end was considerably more sudden and tragic: despite all his success, his continuing mental and emotional struggles, recurring substance abuse, and mounting financial troubles all finally drove him to take his own life in 2014 at age sixty-three.

It's been widely theorized that being diagnosed with

Bob (center) with Robin Williams (left) and Billy Crystal (right) at the wedding of a mutual friend

Parkinson's disease also played a major factor, as Williams couldn't bear to be seen as anything less than the fun-loving, brilliant, whirling dervish that the world had first fallen in love with as Mork from Ork in 1978. I won't speculate further because I didn't know him that well as a person. (Very few did, I believe.) All I know is that during this peak and beyond, nobody from this planet could ever keep up with him—not most of the cast of *Mork*, and not any other comic, including me, who saw it up close and personal week after week.

Doing *Mork* would also not be the last time I would come across Robin Williams. He was a regular guest while I was doing warmup for *The Tonight Show* between 1993 and 2008. During that period, at least, the years had hardly diminished his spirit or energy.

During breaks in the taping, it was customary for most of the *Tonight Show* technical staff to leave the studio to have a cigarette. With Williams there, they were all willing to forgo their nicotine habits to stay and watch what the actor was going to do next. If you took your eyes off Robin Williams for even a second, you might miss something you would later regret.

His passing was a sad and tragic loss of one of the most brilliant comic minds of all time, and I feel honored to have been witness to more than my share of it.

Chapter Six

Taxi

Another aspect of my career in which I take great pride is the fact that in thirty-five years I never cancelled a single warmup gig that I was booked for. Sure there would be scheduling conflicts that needed to be dealt with. But in terms of "calling in," I never did that. Not once, and that includes five times a week on *The Tonight Show* for thirteen years.

And it's not like there was never a reason that I probably should have. I worked on the same day as having laser eye surgery, after a colonoscopy, and even after being in an auto accident. (Nobody was hurt but I ended up taking a cab to the studio, t-shirts in hand.) And those are just the (thankfully) rare occurrences: I got the sniffles (and worse) from time to time like everyone else; I mean, come on, I had a career that involved strangers breathing all over me for three or four hours at a time.

I like to think that part of this has to do with a work ethic. But at the same time one need not be in Hollywood for long to understand a very basic truth: *everyone* is replaceable. This especially goes for warmup comics, since very few of us had any sort of long-term contract with any shows we worked on. Simply put, if you missed a taping and they thought the substitute was better, there's a good chance you wouldn't be coming back to that show anytime soon.

Other warmups, however, would call in sick on occasion—I guess they were either less dedicated or less paranoid than I was—and then I would end up being the one they would call to come fill in.

And while I would certainly never wish ill health on anyone—especially not one of my peers—I have to confess

I was glad that someone else's ailment gave me the chance to work on *Taxi* a few times. This gig didn't mean more money or prestige than I was used to; I simply was (and remain) a huge fan of the show. Working in television doesn't necessarily have to lead you to hate TV, and I could certainly never dislike a show this good.

In fact, it was one of the few times in my career that I was genuinely a bit nervous, not because of the studio audience (they don't differ all that much from show to show, honestly) but rather because I was going to have the chance to witness firsthand the inner workings of one of the best shows on TV at the time (and probably ever).

I was not disappointed. It wasn't customary for me as the warmup comic to be at the rehearsal, for the simple and obvious reason that there was no audience to warm up yet. (Although it is actually a good idea for us to be there so we can get an idea of where the breaks in shooting are, etc. It just doesn't happen that often due to time restrictions.) However, in this case I chose to be there for the rehearsals, if only to simply watch.

Bob addressing a studio audience as Danny DeVito (second from right) looks on

I still considered myself a student of sitcoms as an art form, and in that regard this was Stanford or Brown University. What I witnessed was truly amazing: just that perfect symmetry that was created between the show's top-notch writing and its amazing cast.

And it is sort of astonishing to contemplate just how much talent culminated on this one show. Just for starters, you had Judd Hirsch, who had been a highly respected New York stage actor. And then you had Danny DeVito and Christopher Lloyd, who had both appeared in *One Flew Over the Cuckoo's Nest* and who would each go on to even greater success in feature films.

Bob with Judd Hirsch

Bob with Danny DeVito

Bob with Christopher Lloyd

Bob with Tony Danza

Bob with Marilu Henner

Hirsch was not merely top billing; as far as I could see he was clearly the linchpin that was holding the cast—and by extension the show—together, just as his character, Alex Rieger, held that same position among the characters in the garage of the fictitious Sunshine Cab Company.

There was also Tony Danza, whom I would later spend several years working closely with on his own show, *Who's the Boss?* (see chapter fifteen). Not to mention that the show was cocreated by James L. Brooks, who had been largely responsible for *Mary Tyler Moore* and would later win an Oscar for directing the feature film *Terms of Endearment*. Brooks would also cocreate a little cultural phenomenon known as *The Simpsons*. (Whatever happened to *that* show, anyway?)

On the subject of cultural phenomena, of course there was also Andy Kaufman. Kaufman was billed last in the credits. But even at the time he was already the subject of a cult independent of the show thanks to his act, which was so avant-garde he refused to even call it "comedy." Interest in the performer would grow exponentially after his untimely passing in 1984. Quite a few people actually believe Kaufman faked his own death, although I'm not one of them.

I'd love to describe what it was like watching Kaufman during rehearsal . . . except I can't, because he wasn't there. No, he didn't catch the bug that the regular warmup guy did; apparently Kaufman always skipped rehearsals. Instead, he dispatched a surrogate to say his lines and stand on his marks, a young stand-up comic named Mike Binder.

Binder would go on to direct features films including *Indian Summer, Blankman,* and *The Upside of Anger* as well as act in movies, including *Minority Report*. When standing in for Kaufman, however, Binder spoke in his own natural voice, as opposed to using the character's comically exaggerated foreign accent (except when the dialogue used "words" in the made-up language).

There probably isn't a whole lot to say about Kaufman that isn't covered in Bill Zehme's biography *Lost in the Funhouse* (such as the fact that while he was a star on *Taxi*, Kaufmann had a side-job as a restaurant busboy so that he could observe regular people who usually wouldn't recognize him).

No matter what the specifics of the (many) Kaufmann stories may be (and we'll probably never know), one thing is for certain: even today *Taxi* holds up incredibly well. Watching it now, one is distracted very little by elements that date the show, such as characters fighting over the use of a public phone (or even just the public phone itself).

Doing warmup for *Taxi* might have become "work" if I had done the show more often or on a more permanent basis. But doing it how I did made me feel more like a contest winner who got to hang around the set for a while. I would have loved to do the show more times or even for the whole run, but a short *Taxi* ride was better than no ride at all.

Chapter Seven

Cheers

Cheers was first the hit show I would do warmup for where I had the chance to be there from the very beginning. Most of the time, if you do the pilot you'll be asked to stay with the show. I had been doing *9 to 5* since its inception, but that show only ran for a season (discounting a later syndicated version that I was not involved with). Also, since it was based on a hit movie, with *9 to 5* the series wasn't starting from zero.

Cheers, by contrast, was not based on any existing work. It wasn't a spin-off from another show. It wasn't a thinly-veiled imitation of a hit on another network, or thematically reminiscent of any popular movie (even *Mork & Mindy* indirectly owed its existence to *Star Wars*). Also, it wasn't really even any sort of a reflection of the social climate at the time. There was exactly one motivation behind putting *Cheers* on the air, and that was creating a good show.

This is not to suggest that *Cheers* had nothing going for it when it was originally conceived. It had been the first show from a production company newly formed by James Burrows and brothers Glenn and Les Charles. Burrows was (and would remain) one of the all-time most successful directors in sitcoms going all the way back to *Mary Tyler Moore*, while the Charles brothers had been the creators and producers of *Taxi*.

The general pedigree of the relatively unknown cast, however, was not quite as promising. Shelley Long had appeared alongside Ringo Starr in the movie *Caveman* and had also been the female lead in the Ron Howard comedy *Night Shift*. Ted Danson and most of the rest of the cast had made sporadic appearances on TV or in films. There were no stars, no one on the show whom anyone was going to tune in just to see (apart from their relatives), no real draw to get undecided viewers to watch.

Although the show was to be an ensemble cast, it would also revolve largely around the relationship between the bar owner—an ex-Red Sox pitcher and (ironically) recovering alcoholic—and a waitress who was charming but something of a know-it-all. But the underlying idea was described perfectly in the instantly-classic sing-along theme song: a place "where everybody knows your name." *Cheers* was about a public setting where anyone could become part of a family just by simply being there, which the viewing audience would want to be part of.

The year was 1982. My professional reputation had not yet reached the point where I became everyone's first call when they needed a warmup comic. I would usually be asked to do a show after the producers had seen me doing a different one, and in this case *9 to 5* had been the sitcom that led me to *Cheers*. (I suppose going from a show about an office to one about the kind of place people go after leaving the office was a natural transition.)

For starters, I could certainly appreciate the show's setting, having spent a few years in Boston. I was even well aware of the real-life bar which had been the basis for *Cheers*, the Bull and Finch in the Beacon Hill area. The interior was not used as the model for the *Cheers* set, but the show adopted the idea of the bar being below street level. The outside of the Bull and Finch was also filmed for the exterior shot that opened every episode.

Filming a pilot in front of a live audience is always a bit tricky because the show obviously hasn't aired yet. This means no one attending has seen it, let alone become a fan and developed any sort of investment in the show or the characters. When people watch a pilot at home it's a bit different, since the show is written and edited with the specific intention of leaving viewers wanting more.

However, when filming any sitcom episode live, there are the retakes and breaks between scenes, which make it easy to lose the momentum. So before the first filming of *Cheers*, we tried to fill the gap by having the studio audience watch the original unaired pilot (most programs film one pilot just for the purpose of having something to show the network before shooting the version that will actually run on TV), thus giving everyone a crash course on the plot and characters.

Not all pilot tapings go well—honestly, if anything most *don't* and few of them get picked up. But since *Cheers* was a show about a sports-orientated bar, I'm going to say that this first taping was an unqualified home run. And touchdown. And any other terminology for scoring used in sports (as long as it's not curling . . . I hate curling). It went just that well: between the script and the performances, everyone knew that the show was a winner—including the studio audience, who also reacted as though they had just witnessed a genuine victory.

The ratings, however, threatened to tell a very different story. The first airing not only came in last in its timeslot, it was close to being the lowest-rated show of the entire week. You would think that this news would have deflated what had become the overwhelmingly positive atmosphere defining the set. But as far as I could tell, it did not in the slightest.

It was just like in *How the Grinch Stole Christmas!* when they kept on singing carols in the face of all their gifts having disappeared. You would think *Cheers* had gone right to number one. The reason for this was that everyone from the producer to the grips knew that this was something so truly special it would surely find an audience eventually.

But another part of this optimism probably had to do with the status quo at NBC at the time. Four years earlier, the network hired Fred Silverman as its president. Silverman was considered a programming genius who in the preceding decade had led each of the other networks to the top (on separate occasions, obviously).

Silverman, as it turned out, would have the reverse effect

on the peacock network, his tenure marred by what-is-this-guy-smoking programming choices like *Supertrain* and *Hello, Larry*. (A *Saturday Night Live* sketch at the time portrayed Silverman as a double agent, still employed by ABC to bring NBC down from the inside. It almost seemed plausible.)

Possibly Silverman's most notorious failure had been developing a variety show vehicle for Pink Lady, a female singing duo who were all the rage in their native Japan. Considerable money and resources were already sunk into the project before it was discovered that the girls didn't speak English. Six catastrophic episodes were produced with the two girls reciting lines that they had to learn phonetically.

With virtually nothing left to lose, NBC began an unofficial policy of putting quality shows on the air and then giving them time to find an audience. (*Hill Street Blues* and *St. Elsewhere* were two such shows that would benefit from this practice.) As such, *Cheers* was not too concerned about the weak ratings—yet. They were aware that they still only get so much rope. Perhaps no one was yet predicting that the show would be around for eleven years, but everyone figured we were safe in the short run.

Actually, the producers seemed only interested in beating one show in particular: *Family Ties*, a sitcom that had started at about the same time and was taping at the next studio over. The shows were not in direct competition since they were both on NBC. However, being in such close proximity, the sitcoms became sort of like two roommates who were both competing for the Olympics. A degree of the general mood on the *Cheers* set would inevitably fluctuate according to whether or not it beat *Family Ties* any given week.

A different headache would also surface—this one from within. By the third episode, I had already developed a rhythm as far as knowing about how much time I would be interacting with the audience between scenes. However, I was thrown a small curveball during that third episode when the stage manager gave me the signal to "stretch," meaning I had to keep going because they weren't ready yet to start filming again.

I assumed it was some kind of a technical problem, not uncommon during TV tapings. But at the end of the very next scene, I was getting the exact same signal from the stage manager. By now I'm starting to wonder what could possibly be causing another delay this soon.

It turned out not to be a technical problem at all. Rather, Shelley Long was taking longer and longer to have her hair and makeup done before every scene, even those which she would only appear in briefly. Not a *touch-up*, which is usually done throughout filming anyway, but the *full* hair and makeup that is supposed to be gotten out of the way before the shoot begins (in order to make the process quicker).

From the beginning, the set had been running a relatively tight ship—filming usually took about three hours. But what Long had asked for (and gotten) was now adding at least an hour every week. Between scenes, when everyone knew that this was what was causing the holdup, you could tell just by looking at the faces of the other actors while they waited—on the set and in costume—that they were not at all happy about this.

Luckily, when Long did finally emerge there was no denying how strong the chemistry between her and Danson was on camera, as well as between the entire cast. And of course in terms of the delays, the home viewers were never any the wiser.

After two seasons I stopped regularly doing warmup for *Cheers*. I wasn't having any problems with the production; I just felt it was time to move on. However, I did come back periodically for the rest of the show's run. During future tapings I would have the chance to observe some of the great talent—including Woody Harrelson, Kelsey Grammer, and Bebe Neuwirth—who would join the cast later.

And of course there was also Kirstie Alley, who joined the show at the beginning of the sixth season after Shelley Long left to pursue her (ultimately unsuccessful) film career. Although Alley became the female lead, she didn't quite replace Long since the character was so noticeably different—a credit to the show for not simply trying to recreate the same formula, or even just recast the role a la *Bewitched*.

While I know it's not the common opinion, I honestly always thought that the show was better after Alley joined. I preferred the chemistry that she had with Danson and the rest of the cast and also felt that her sense of comedic timing was an improvement over her predecessor's. And throughout the Alley years the show's ratings would remain either as good or better.

Cheers would spend a decade in a much-deserved top ten position beginning in the fall of 1984, when *The Cosby Show* became the lead-off for the Thursday prime-time lineup, sending the ratings of every show on that night (including *Family Ties*) skyrocketing. Ironically, in the process, *Cosby* would destroy a show that I had far more extensive involvement with—more on that later.

But regardless of where they ended up in the Nielsens, the show about the bar "where everybody knows your name" would always prove to be a near-perfect cocktail of acting, writing, humanity, and characterization that I was very happy to have been a part of (and from the beginning, no less). Cheers, indeed.

Chapter Eight

Newhart

In my three and a half decades of doing audience warmup, it never ceased to amaze me how many sitcom stars truly did not understand the dynamic of doing a show with members of the general public in attendance. A few cases were worse than others, as some actors would eventually adapt while others never would. But thanks to editing—and inevitably a laugh track—home viewers were (usually) none the wiser.

But some stars never even *tried*, and their attitude would gradually corrode the show until the whole thing became unsalvageable. In the course of my career I would watch more than one sitcom crash and burn under these circumstances.

What I witnessed doing *Newhart* was the polar opposite of what I just described: that show's star, Bob Newhart, understood perfectly what his relationship with the studio audience needed to be in order to make every taping, and in turn the whole show, successful.

At least part of this can be attributed to experience: beyond Newhart's career as one of the most popular stand-up comedians of the early Sixties, he also had *The Bob Newhart Show* to his credit. That series had been part of the original wave of early Seventies sitcoms, along with *Mary Tyler Moore*, *All in the Family*, and *Sanford and Son*, to reject laugh tracks and bring back live audiences (and in the process assuring that someone like me would have a career).

The early part of my warmup career became sort of a professional chain of events, and I was hired to do *Newhart* after their producers had watched me doing *Cheers*. I did *Newhart* from the pilot in 1982 until I left to become story editor on *Who's the Boss?* in 1988, although I did return to *Newhart* for the final episode. (I would've kicked myself if I hadn't been there for *that*.)

Newhart was always openly opposed to laugh tracks, and while I wasn't involved with post-production on the show, I know that he also wanted to keep sweetening (the term for laughs that are added or edited on a show that uses a live audience) to a bare minimum.

At the beginning of every taping (and in eight years I only missed a couple due to the occasional scheduling conflict), I would come out among the audience and introduce myself before directing their attention to Newhart as he walked out on the stage. He would then tell the audience a joke, usually the same one about a parrot that spoke only after his owner had failed to feed him (he might throw in a few other ones, usually from his original stand-up routines), before taking some questions from the audience members and otherwise addressing a few of them individually.

Once the actual shooting began a few minutes later, Newhart was rarely in plain sight if he wasn't being filmed. When not needed on the set, he would spend most of his time somewhere backstage—usually doing crossword puzzles, which were his favorite leisure activity.

Crosswords require a fair amount of knowledge, but at least one thing Newhart clearly understood was just how much that little extra effort on his part at the beginning of every taping was worth. He realized that this was not like doing a stage play or even a real-time show like *Saturday Night Live*.

Rather, what we had here was a studio audience that was about to be asked to sit through reshoots and what could turn into long breaks between scenes—and most people who attend sitcom tapings really have no idea what they're getting themselves into.

So even though we had about a three-hour process ahead of us, Newhart in those ten minutes or so had done about half my job for me. From this point on, it was still up to me to keep the audience in the good graces of everything that would transpire, and in the mood to laugh. But the difference was that I wasn't the one they'd come to see. The star of the show had just extended an effort to make a personal connection with them. This made all the difference.

Ironically, a few episodes in, Newhart called for a change that was purely in regard to the home viewers. The show was originally shot on video rather than on film. Most sitcom viewers can easily spot the difference: videotape is the clearer, more realistic-looking format.

After watching what's referred to in the business as "the dailies" (which, as the name would suggest, means reviewing footage shot that same day), Newhart decided that on videotape he simply looked a bit *older* than he wanted to. So he immediately had the tapes transferred to film (and then eventually the show would simply be shot in that format).

This wasn't the only change to occur early in the show's run. Two members of the supporting cast, Steven Kampmann and Jennifer Holmes, who played Kirk Devane and Leslie Vanderkellen respectively, would be dropped from *Newhart* by the end of the second season. As far as I found out, neither of them proved to be unprofessional in any way or fell victim to backstage politics; they simply weren't the right fit for the show.

It was a whole different story when Julia Duffy joined the cast in the third season. She was instantly hilarious as Stephanie Vanderkellen (the previous character's cousin), an heiress who'd been reduced to working as a chambermaid yet somehow would never be humbled by her new surroundings and continued to act like a spoiled brat.

Some people might have assumed that Duffy herself was the same way, but in actuality she was nothing like her character: she was always pleasant, friendly, and a consummate team player; not remotely self-centered either as an actress or as a person.

Tom Poston, on the other hand, was a lot more like his character George Utley: docile, soft-spoken, and humble. This had been my second time working with Poston, as he had been a supporting player on *Mork & Mindy*. He and I became friends outside of the studio, and I was even invited to his house in the San Fernando Valley a couple of times.

Then there was Mary Frann, who played Joanna, the wife of Newhart's character Dick Loudon. This role, I felt, never had all that much depth; she was mainly there for the purpose of being just "the wife." However, this was probably necessary because the type of character Newhart played wouldn't really have worked as an unmarried man. (This is absolutely nothing against Frann, who also was always extremely professional and gracious and never at all jaded.)

In fact, the only negative experience I ever had with an actor while doing *Newhart* involved one who wasn't even on the show. During a third season taping, William Sanderson, who played the character Larry (more on him in a minute) called me to one side and told me he had a friend sitting in the audience, a celebrity whom he wanted me to introduce to the crowd.

It turned out to be David Naughton, who first became famous in the late Seventies singing and dancing in a series of iconic commercials for Dr. Pepper soda ("Be a Pepper"). Around that time, he also starred on a Garry Marshall sitcom, *Makin' It*; the show only lasted a couple of months but the theme song, which Naughton sang, became a top five hit. Today, he's probably best remembered as the star of the 1981 feature film *An American Werewolf in London*.

I complied with Sanderson's request and gave Naughton a big, praiseful introduction, after which the crowd responded warmly. Moments later, Naughton, sitting in his seat, caught my eye and gestured for me to come over to him.

Filming had just resumed, so Naughton understood that he had to whisper to me . . . but he did so in the most unmistakably indignant whisper I ever heard. He demanded to know how *dare* I do that without asking him first and that it had better *never* happen again. Taken aback, I tried to explain that it was his personal friend, a cast member, who had asked me to do it, and I apologized.

A couple of years later, Naughton would have a supporting role on the sitcom *My Sister Sam*. Although I did warmup for that show a couple of times, I didn't end up having any direct interaction with him. My next up-close-and-personal encounter with the man was around 2000 at a Hollywood party, during which I ordered a drink from him: David Naughton was there tending bar.

Despite his being rude to me on the *Newhart* set years earlier, at the party I took the high ground and abstained from rubbing salt in Naughton's wounds: I *didn't* joke that I wanted to order a Dr. Pepper (as I'll bet half the people he waited on did). But it just goes to show that working in entertainment you can never take your success for granted.

The cast that would propel *Newhart* into the stratosphere of classic sitcoms would not be fully in place until the third season, with the addition of Peter Scolari. This would become the third show I would work on with Scolari in less than five years, following *Goodtime Girls* (a short-lived series set in the Forties) and my few times doing *Bosom Buddies* (on which he costarred with Tom Hanks).

I had mixed feelings when I found out that Scolari was joining the cast of *Newhart*. On the one hand, he was a friend, and as an actor he was an asset to any show. At the same time, however, Scolari always had one personal trait that never sat particularly well with me.

Specifically, Peter Scolari was a juggler. No, I don't mean metaphorically. The man was, in fact, a professional juggler. Now, I recognize that this is a legitimate skill that takes years of training and practice to be able to do at the level that Scolari did. But personally, I've always felt about jugglers the way I do about mimes. Which, in turn, is the way nearly everyone feels about mimes: that they're annoying, pretty much superfluous as a form of entertainment, and more than a bit disturbing.

When we did *Goodtime Girls*, the writers had been able to work this hidden talent of Scolari's into the scripts. However, on *Newhart* he played Michael Harris, a typical

Eighties yuppie whose concern was for little besides career advancement, so the juggling would've been out of character. But Scolari still needed to get his juggle on somehow, so he decided to seize the fact that while doing Newhart he would have a live audience at his disposal once a week.

Like any professional juggler, Scolari never dropped anything. Yet at every taping, I knew one thing was inevitably going to drop: the proverbial second shoe, which in this case came in the form of Scolari calling me to one side and quietly asking if it was okay for him to do some juggling for the audience while we were all waiting for the crew to set up the next scene.

He would already have his props in hand, usually bowling pins (which even I recognized as a juggling cliché). To be fair, Scolari did always ask me first, and he never tried to pull and any kind of rank as a cast member. But after several dozen times, he also probably realized I wasn't going to say anything other than "Sure, go right ahead."

Scolari's juggling would be met by scattered "oohs" and "ahhs" for the first few seconds before the novelty wore off. It was probably just the wrong atmosphere to display that sort of skill, the same way these people wouldn't have gone to the circus to hear jokes.

Contending with a few minutes of this every week was a small price to pay for the assemblage of what was now clearly a first-rate sitcom cast. More and more episodes even began to focus on some of these secondary characters rather than Newhart's. Whether it was because he had nothing left to prove at this point in his career or because his name was already the show's entire title, Newhart was always fully behind this. Critics began to praise him for allowing "his" program to evolve into this ensemble piece.

One thing that I would do with the audience at every taping was select one person to get up and sing. The song would always be "New York, New York." This was before karaoke machines—with screens displaying the lyrics—were commercially available, so I picked this tune because I figured most people already know the words to it.

Even karaoke *tapes*—with just the music and no vocals—weren't really available yet, so I brought in a boom box along with a tape of Frank Sinatra's original recording of the song. I would single out someone from the crowd, put a trench coat and fedora hat on them, and have them sing along with Sinatra's vocal.

Whenever I did these audience participation things, I would usually either ask for a volunteer or look for someone that I could guess would be a good sport; it was never my intention to embarrass anyone. But this whole simple, fairly innocent stunt led to another incident that potentially could have meant a bit of embarrassment for me.

For reasons that I still can't possibly imagine, while Newhart was somewhere backstage (most likely doing a crossword) he heard the song and always assumed that what he was hearing was *me* serenading the crowd! I have no idea why he thought that. I'm not a singer. Most professional actors can at least carry a tune (in case they ever have to do a stage musical) but I'm not one of them. Furthermore, I don't believe I ever said anything to imply to Newhart that I was any kind of a professional crooner.

That Christmas, I was invited to a sit-down dinner at Newhart's house. Some of the other guests included Ed McMahon, Don Rickles (who was one of Newhart's best friends), Burt Bacharach, and Katherine Helmond, among many others.

As close as I was to big stars on a daily basis, I wasn't that used to sitting among this many of them all at once, and as their equal—or at least the guy at the end of the table who put ketchup on his steak. So while I had a very good personal relationship with Newhart and everyone at the party seemed down-to-earth enough, it was still already just a bit overwhelming.

After dinner, we all went into the living room, where some of the guests were invited to get up in front of everyone for an impromptu performance. With this much talent present, it would be almost unthinkable not to do this. Rickles got

Bob with Don Rickles

up and told a couple of jokes. There was also a grand piano in the room, so Bacharach went over and played a couple of songs.

Then Newhart approached me and asked, "Bob, why don't you get up there and sing 'New York, New York' like you do at the tapings every week?"

I was taken aback. Someone thought I had been singing when I actually wasn't! I knew, at that moment, how Milli Vanilli felt. Do I simply explain everything to Newhart now about the boom box and the Sinatra tape and everything? No. That night Newhart was my host, and it may have seemed ungracious to simply refuse the request. Also, despite how many iconic figures were there that night, it was still all pretty informal. So I decided to go up and simply do it.

Bacharach, still at the piano (at least someone was squarely in his element), began playing the song. As I kept trying to figure out how I was going to approach the whole thing, it became more and more obvious that I was hesitating.

Luckily, Newhart had the answer: he sent two of his other guests, the legendary singing duo of Steve Lawrence and Eydie Gorme, up to help me. At first I jokingly told them, "Hey! I work alone!" This got a big laugh and then the three of us ended up doing the song.

While it may not have quite been a sit-down dinner with Steve and Eydie, back on the *Newhart* set there was routinely a small after-party with pizza and soda once each episode wrapped. On some shows I worked on, as soon as taping was done the star would practically run out of the studio as though it were on fire. But Newhart almost always stuck around for these gatherings, showing his cast and crew at the end of the taping the same consideration he had showed the studio audience at the beginning.

During its eight-year run *Newhart* had probably two defining moments, and I'm proud to have been there while both were filmed. The first was the introduction of three hugely popular characters by their catchphrase: "Hi, I'm Larry, that's my brother Darryl, and that's my *other* brother Darryl."

The five-thousandth time you hear these words, they're still pretty funny. But when originally the line was uttered on the show by William Sanderson, who played Larry, in his deadpan drawl, the audience continued to laugh for so long that the take finally became unusable and they had to yell "cut."

After that successful debut appearance, the three became recurring characters until they were finally made full regulars in the third season. So popular was the trio that many people, in order to differentiate this series from *The Bob Newhart Show*, will still refer to *Newhart* as "the one with Larry, Darryl, and Darryl."

Of the three, only Larry ever spoke; part of the joke was

that the other two were seemingly mute. As such, Tony Papenfuss and John Voldstad, who played the Darryls (as they were sometimes referred to collectively), were asked by the producers never to speak out loud in front of the studio audience, even after the taping had wrapped.

It wasn't quite a Harpo Marx situation: both actors had done, and continued to do, other roles where they did speak. And during nearly any sitcom taping, the audience will generally see an actor out of character more than in. However, recognizing the iconic status that their creations had now reached, Papenfuss and Voldstad agreed to remain silent for the entire process so that the illusion could be at least somewhat maintained.

Mute characters always promise a sort of comedic jack-in-the-box: there's inevitably a killer gag waiting to emerge in both when they finally talk and what it is they actually say. In fact, Barry Kemp, one of the show's producers, even told *TV Guide* in 1987 that the Darryls at last speaking might just be the climactic gag of the show's last episode.

As it turned out, in the final installment the characters *did* finally speak, a single word ("Quiet!") in unison. But it was not the gag that ended the series. What ultimately transpired as the finale of *Newhart* trumped even that, or anything else anyone could have imagined.

A couple of years earlier, Patrick Duffy (no relation to Julia) had wished to return to the nighttime soap *Dallas* following a one-year absence. Just one problem: his character had died. So while the writers probably could have come up with a half-dozen ways to resurrect him (not that any of them would've been plausible), they decided instead to reveal that the entire season during which he had supposedly been dead had been a dream. Critics and fans alike called this the biggest cop-out ever.

So in 1990, as *Newhart* was winding down, they decided to top this by revealing that not only had the entire *series* been a dream but that it had been dreamt by Dr. Robert Hartley, Newhart's character from his previous sitcom!

The icing on the cake would be that Suzanne Pleshette, who played Hartley's wife, Emily, on that last show, agreed to come on *Newhart* to be part of this gag. On the day of the taping, lest the surprise be spoiled, she had to be snuck in the back of the studio and then remain hidden as much as possible.

I had been gone from the proceedings for about two years by that point, but I had been asked back to do the final episode. But I had not been let in on the big twist ahead of time, and like everyone else in the audience (and later the home audience) I could not have imagined just what was in store.

At that taping, there was even a curtain that was placed in front of the set until they were ready to film. Once "action" was called and the lights came on for this final scene, a few audience members already recognized what was meant to look like the bedroom set from *The Bob Newhart Show* (although it was not, in fact, the original set, which presumably had long since been dismantled).

Newhart was lying in a double bed, where there was clearly another person beneath the covers; a faint moan then came from that mysterious lump. Pleshette had a fairly distinct voice, so the anticipation level rose even further as more members of the audience began to get an idea of where this was going. But when the lights came on and Pleshette turned around, now making her fully visible, my jaw dropped along with everyone else's. The full response from the studio audience at that point, as I'm sure they predicted, was just overwhelming.

Over the years I had done warmup for quite a few "final episodes" (particularly when you include tapings where they didn't realize it would be the last show of the series). This one, however, was already especially bittersweet, the culmination of eight years of work between people who had essentially become a family: I watched as tough-as-nails teamsters (members of the crew) began weeping openly. The whole "dream" element in this final scene added an almost otherworldly dimension, the idea that it had somehow all not been real.

Wait—does this mean that as the warmup guy for *Newhart*, I was only part of the dream, too? I certainly hope not. (I already cashed all the checks.) Doing the warmup for six years of *Newhart* was a pleasure and an honor. Helmed by talented people who genuinely understood how a sitcom needed to be approached in order to truly work, it was the kind of experience that warmup guys dream about.

Chapter Nine

Oh, Madeline

Madeline Kahn was a popular and hugely talented comedic actress. She had a very distinct persona that combined her elegant beauty with a (genuine) quirky speech pattern characterized by what's called a "lazy s." Kahn was probably best known for her memorable appearances in Mel Brooks' back-to-back classics *Blazing Saddles* and *Young Frankenstein*. All this, and she was even a gifted singer.

In theory, a sitcom probably seemed like a perfect—even obvious—vehicle for Madeline Kahn. This is what ABC was banking on when *Oh, Madeline* debuted in 1983 as one of the network's highly-touted new fall shows. It would also be the first series produced by a company just formed by Tom Werner and Marcy Carsey, who as ABC executives had been closely involved with *Happy Days*, *Soap*, *Taxi*, and *Bosom Buddies*, among other shows. (They've also publicly taken credit for casting Robin Williams as Mork, although this claim has been widely disputed.)

Thirteen episodes of *Oh, Madeline* were produced, and I did the warmup for all of them. Yet at every single taping, before cameras even began rolling, I could spot a serious and potentially detrimental problem which had surfaced. Actually, it was something—or rather somebody—that *failed* to surface when they really should have.

Nearly all sitcom tapings start out with the main cast being brought out and introduced to the crowd. In the last chapter I described how Bob Newhart would open his show by coming out and telling jokes to the audience for a few minutes. This endeared him to the crowd, who would now be rooting for him (and by extension his costars) right from the word "action."

Madeline Kahn, however, did not want to come out and greet the crowd—not even for just a moment—at the beginning of any of the tapings of her show. A number of people on the set would attempt to coax her, but to no avail. Since she was not just the star but a well-known film actress, one might assume somehow that this was the result of "diva" behavior. However, nothing I saw for the remainder of any of the tapings—where she was always professional and courteous to everyone—would support that theory.

Actors, as most people know, have a lot of personal superstitions (i.e., saying "break a leg" instead of "good luck"), so it's entirely possible that Kahn had such a fear that kept her from coming out at the beginning of the show. She also had almost no previous sitcom experience (another general problem), so it's also possible that she assumed it was

Bob with Madeline Kahn

going to be like live theater and that if the audience saw her as "herself" they would not be able to accept her as the character (even though it was pretty consistent with the persona that everyone was already familiar with).

I actually never found out her reason. All I know is that it hurt the show and set off the downhill trajectory of not just each individual taping but the entire series. Now you may well be thinking, "Oh, come on! How much difference could it possibly make if the star doesn't want to come out and *wave* to the crowd before the taping begins? Aren't they supposed to be there for the jokes, anyway?" Well, I will explain, if you'd care to indulge me.

A sitcom taping with a studio audience is not like live theater. If you go to watch a stage presentation—whether it's on Broadway, or a local production a la *Waiting for Guffman*, or even a high school play—the people putting the show on are creating an illusion for you. They do this with the script and the performances, and maybe music and special effects, which are all you are going to see (and hear) once the house lights go down.

By contrast, if you go to a live sitcom taping, you're going to see far, far more than just what's eventually going to end up on your TV screen—whether you want to or not. This includes (but probably won't be limited to) multiple retakes, actors stepping out of character, obtrusive technical equipment (and technicians) everyplace you look, and writers appearing out of nowhere to "fix" the script (supposedly) on-the-fly. Plus an annoying warmup guy. (*Me?* Sure, sometimes.) Not to mention long periods when nothing happens on the stage for no apparent reason (although the reason is usually that the directors take however long a break as they feel like).

So in effect, the audience for a sitcom taping is not there to enjoy a performance as much as they are to be part of the process. This is not to suggest that nobody has a good time sitting in the audience for a sitcom—most people have a very good time and relish getting to watch a work in progress in addition to laughing at the (hopefully) funny stuff.

However, sitcom audiences are largely composed of tourists from out of town, and there's nothing to prepare them for what they're about to sit through. There are no "regional sitcoms" being taped in Indiana. There's no sitcom road company that makes stops in Nebraska and Idaho. So most people who come to watch sitcom tapings are largely unprepared for what they're about to experience.

This is why it's so important for someone like Bob Newhart to come out and address the audience before the taping begins. Although he's telling jokes, the message that he's essentially sending them is: "For the next three hours or so, we're all in this together." Newhart may be a gifted comic, but I've found that just about any actor can be as effective if they make that little extra human-touch effort.

At the same time, even casual sitcom viewers are aware of what's called "sweetening," where even though a live audience is used, "laughs" will be punched-up or added during post-production. And I've already discussed at least one incident where the reaction of the studio audience turned out to be almost 100 percent unusable and had to be completely replaced with an artificial laugh track.

So then how can the audience—and establishing that sort of bond with them—still be that important? Well, when the actors are performing, there's a rhythm that the audience creates that is essential. If the collective attitude of the audience deteriorates, that of everyone else usually goes right along with it. Actors and writers start thinking, at least on some subconscious level: "Hmmm . . . I guess maybe we're *not* funny." Plus, in spite of everything else, they are still fundamentally performing for the people in the studio audience.

This is what the experience of being present for well over a thousand sitcom taping tells me, anyway.

All that said, Kahn's aversion to "meeting" the audience up front alone did not do *Oh, Madeline* in. It simply wasn't a very good show, not in terms of dialogue, story, structuring, or the performances (other than Kahn's). The final episode aired that March.

Bob acting in an episode of Oh, Madeline

By no stretch of the imagination was this the end of the line for Madeline Kahn. And definitely not for Carsey-Werner Productions; just six months later they would produce *The Cosby Show*, which would eventually become the most successful TV show of all time. The company would also have major hits with shows like *Roseanne, Grace Under Fire*, and *3rd Rock from the Sun*. (In 2001 Werner bought a sizeable share of the Boston Red Sox.)

Madeline Kahn would continue to work consistently in film, theater, and television. She even ended up on not just another sitcom but another Carsey-Werner sitcom, with a supporting role on Bill Cosby's late-Nineties vehicle titled simply *Cosby*. *Oh, Madeline* would pretty much fall by the wayside, which is actually a good thing: Kahn, who died in 1999, deserves to be remembered for her better work.

Chapter Ten

Night Court

By late 1983, when I began working on *Night Court*, I was at the point where I had proven to sitcom producers and even myself that doing audience warmup didn't mean you were just a glorified usher, or that all I did for four hours was ask audience members where they were from. Rather, what I was doing had its own integrity and had become an important, if not crucial part of the show.

With that in mind, and in an effort to keep it fresh, I decided to take it to the next level. With the assistance of the very able tech crew and the show's star (who was helpful to me above and beyond), I was able to create what essentially became an entire pre-show just for the *Night Court* studio audience.

The crowd for the night's typical taping would be seated. Then, rather than me simply coming out to greet them as I had been doing on most shows, their attention would be directed to the video monitors that were set up (the main purpose of which was to provide the studio audience an unobstructed view during the actual show). On the screen was a live feed: it was me backstage, where I would be sitting on a bench and looking like someone had just let the air out of my tires.

Harry Anderson, the star of the show, already in his costume as Judge Harry Stone, would then walk up to me.

"What's the matter, Bob?" he would ask.

"It's the audience, Harry," I would sigh. At that point, I'd always hear a slight-but-audible murmur from the studio—we had gotten everyone's attention. Then I'd tell him: "I just don't feel like they're into it tonight."

This would be the cue for the audience to cheer or yell "Yes, we are!" which they always unfailingly did. Harry would pause and say, "Did you hear that?" and they'd cheer even louder. Then, he'd begin addressing them directly, saying right into the camera: "Come on, you can do better than that!" or "Hey, let's really help Bob out if you want to have a good time tonight!"

At that point, one of us would say, "Maybe some music would help!" A song would begin playing, and I would do either a dance or some other routine along with the tune. For a while my go-to song was David Lee Roth's version of "Just a Gigolo/I Ain't Got Nobody," which was a hit in 1985. A stagehand would hand me a top hat and cane, or a toy saxophone, and I'd be on my way.

Today, pulling this off would be far less involved: I'd really only have to bring the songs in as digital tracks on my smartphone. But back then I had to rely on the sound engineers, who in this case were actually situated in a van that was outside the studio.

I was always very fortunate that these technicians, who already had enough to do with the "real" show, agreed to help me like this. They weren't getting paid extra for doing so, and I was cutting into what was supposed to have been their "down time." As always, I tried to make it so much fun that they would enjoy getting to play a more creative role in the show than they might have otherwise.

I had hundreds of songs on eight-track tapes (yup, *again* with those ancient artifacts), which I would carry to the studio in a large canvas bag. And carry it I did—this was before someone had the genius idea to put wheels on the things. When I got there and went into the van, I would have to dump them on the floor (the sound guys always seemed to be okay with this, to their further credit) and go through them until I found the right songs and sound effects cues that I might want to use that night.

Just as I used songs other than the Roth track, I also didn't just do "What's the matter, Bob?" week after week. I came up with variations. Sometimes we would open with me lying on the floor pretending to be unconscious ("Oh no! Bob's dead! We can't do the show!"), then my cohorts would tell the audience that the only way I could be revived would be if the audience would make more noise. (Okay, so I stole that one from Tinkerbell.)

One thing that unfortunately never occurred to me was to *film* any of those opening skits, as I could not have imagined that there would someday be such a thing as YouTube or that entire seasons of *Night Court* would be commercially released as DVD sets, where they would have made great bonus material. (Not to mention make a couple of extra bucks for yours truly. By the way, thanks again for buying this book.)

These bits served two general purposes: 1) They would formally introduce me, their warmup guy, to the crowd, and 2) they would make the audience feel like they were part of the proceedings. But once we were done with this part, I would come out and then we would begin the real show, with *Night Court* officially ready to begin another session.

The show was created by Reinhold Weege, who had previously worked on the ABC sitcom *Barney Miller* (another of my all-time favorites, although I was never involved with it myself), which was set in a New York City police precinct and known for mixing some drama with its outlandish but plausible comedic stories.

Though *Night Court* was not technically a spin-off, it did sort of take up where the other show left off: if you were arrested by the cops in *Barney Miller*'s precinct, your next stop may well be in front of Judge Harry Stone in the night court.

Both shows utilized the setting of New York City in the Seventies and Eighties, a period when the Big Apple had a major worm in it, being just as weird as it was dangerous. *Night Court* only really maintained that same tone at the beginning, however, and would lean increasingly towards slapstick and surreal humor as it went on.

Harry Anderson first came to national attention for his

work as a magician. He did his act a number of times on *Saturday Night Live*, sporting the glasses and a fedora that had become his "look." The producers of *Cheers* decided to work the basic persona into a recurring role for him as con man Harry the Hat (like the great Lucille Ball, Anderson had a name that apparently seemed so fitting it would be used for most of his characters).

Anderson altered his look a bit for the character on *Night Court* (though the fedora would often resurface when Stone wasn't wearing his judge's robe). He would later say there had been some concern that viewers wouldn't accept him as a judge after he had played a con man, but those worries quickly proved to be unwarranted.

In person, Anderson was every bit as friendly and cordial as he always seemed to be on camera. Just one example: During this time a production company was looking to create a show around me (yes, *me*), that would have been a sort of man-on-the-street program. Anderson, on his own time, came down to the studio and recorded a short video endorsing the project for us to use. We didn't pay him and he had no other stake in it. He did this all strictly as a personal favor (though, sadly, even with his help we never sold the new show).

The other dominant figure on *Night Court* was unquestionably John Larroquette, who played opportunistic-but-lovable assistant district attorney Dan Fielding. (The role would ultimately win the actor four Emmys.) Up until then, Larroquette was probably best known for the Bill Murray military farce *Stripes*, where he played an officer (whose assistant happened to have been played by John Voldstad, a.k.a. Darryl #2 from *Newhart . . . in a speaking role!*).

As his character was something of a lady-killer and man-about-town, some might find it surprising that in real life Larroquette was a major technology geek. He owned personal computers long before they were commonplace and would often come to the set describing "how many gigs" (which most people even *now* don't realize is short for "gigabytes") the machines had, or using other cyber-jargon that absolutely none of the rest of us understood at the time. (Except maybe Phil, the show's grip. *Don't ask*.)

In his public life Larroquette was always very open about his alcoholism; he was nearly two years sober when *Night Court* began. The actor was also dedicated to helping others dealing with the same situation: I once overheard him saying to one of our guest stars who—from what I heard of the conversation—may have been struggling with trying to stay on the wagon: "You can call me any time, day or night." This is when I started to have a great deal of respect for John Larroquette.

Anderson and Larroquette emerged as the show's two stars. *Night Court* was (and was always intended to be) an ensemble cast, although until about halfway through the show's run there would be something of a revolving door. Cast changes, as they usually do, happened for a variety of reasons.

During the first season, Karen Austin had been cast as Lana Wagner, the pretty young court clerk who was also a possible romantic interest for Harry Stone. It would be a tremendous understatement to say that her brief time on the show ended badly. One taping day she seemed even less happy than usual with her screen time for that episode. She had always been quite brazen about having considered herself to be the show's costar.

The tension finally boiled up to a point at which she physically attacked Anderson. This all happened about an hour before I got there, but once I arrived everyone's first words were, "Did you hear what happened?" I would actually (to this day, in fact) hear conflicting stories that she stabbed him in the thigh with a pencil and threw a cup of cold coffee at him. What's pretty much *not* in dispute, however, is that Austin immediately ended up having to be bodily removed from the studio by security.

Perhaps in an effort to get the bad taste of that experience out of their mouths, producers went in a completely different direction when creating a new character for the court clerk, casting thirty-five-year-old actor Charles Robinson.

Robinson was a very nice man and people who only saw him on the show, where he looked a bit chunky and his character usually walked slowly and wore old-man sweaters, might be surprised to learn that he had been a very active fitness enthusiast.

Most of the cast members were always happy to come out and speak directly to the studio audience between scenes, answering their questions or just interacting with them on a personal level. Anderson, however, refrained from ever doing his magic act for the crowd, probably since they were able to work it into the show and his character (in contrast to Peter Scolari's compulsive desire to juggle for the *Newhart* crowd).

The only cast member I was never particularly fond of was Richard Moll, who played the bailiff Bull Shannon for the show's entire run. At six-foot-seven Moll was designated as the gentle giant, but off-camera the "gentle" part usually flew

Bob with cast members (left to right) Richard Moll, Selma Diamond, and Harry Anderson

right out the window. I always found Moll to be unpleasant and needlessly abrasive, and in the years since he's expressed open distain for the show and the cast, stating vehemently that he'd never do any sort of a reunion. (Talk about ungrateful— if not for *Night Court*, he'd probably be walking around today as a giant costumed mascot at some theme park.)

Though never officially a cast member, another figure who would have an undeniable presence on the show was jazz singer Mel Tormé. The "Velvet Fog," as he was known, was name-dropped incessantly in early episodes as being Harry's favorite musician. As Tormé was very much alive and well at the time, it was probably inevitable that he would turn up on the show at some point.

Throughout my career I've always found veteran entertainers, in person, to be a mixed bag: many are extremely pleasant but quite a few are extremely bitter, still angry over career snafus that they experienced many years earlier. So in this instance, since the whole idea was pretty much introduced to illustrate

Bob with Mel Tormé

just how un-hip Harry was, one might have expected Tormé to be resentful, or feel that he had been reduced to a punch-line after decades of hard work.

This, as it turns out, was not the case at all. Going back to his first time on the show, Tormé openly expressed that he was "thrilled" to be among us. He would eventually return for eight subsequent—equally pleasant—appearances. And it was mutually beneficial; the singer would later say that many younger people found out who he was and discovered his music because of the show.

Mel Tormé wasn't the only one who enjoyed his days on *Night Court*. Eight years on the show very much agreed with me as well, between the amazing cast and all-around jovial atmosphere (not to mention that I wrote one episode). My final verdict on *Night Court*: definitely among the highlights of my career.

Chapter Eleven

People Do the Craziest Things

Let me ask you something: Did you ever see *Bambi Meets Godzilla*? If you're not familiar with it, no, I'm not making it up. It's a classic 1969 animated short by Marv Newland. Less than two minutes long, it begins with Bambi grazing in the forest as the opening credits roll. Just as soon as the credits are done, Godzilla's giant foot comes out from the top of the screen and crushes Bambi to death. *The End.*

David Mamet already used this analogy as the basis for a book about Hollywood, but we're going to co-opt it here because it's just so fitting. What happens to Bambi is pretty much what happened to the first network show I ever did where I was on camera, *People Do the Craziest Things*. It was 1984, and the show was scheduled opposite *The Cosby Show* and *Magnum, P. I.* Designated to be my first big break, it ended up being my first big *heart*break instead.

Craziest Things was a basic hidden camera show, meant to catch the reactions of average people in odd situations who didn't know they were being filmed. This concept had been a TV stalwart beginning with *Candid Camera* way back in 1948. (I would do an "official" version of that show a few years later. More on that soon.)

Earlier in 1984, NBC managed a rating success with a midseason replacement show, *TV's Bloopers and Practical Jokes* starring Dick Clark and Ed McMahon. Most of the show was composed of outtakes from TV shows (those would be the "bloopers"), but each episode also included two segments where a hidden camera stunt was pulled on an unsuspecting celebrity.

Thus, hidden camera shows proving once again to be a safe bet, *People Do the Craziest Things* moved forward. Bert Convy was recruited as the host: he was a pleasant, amiable actor who had been seen in a couple of feature films (*Hero at Large, The Cannonball Run*) but was mainly known for his TV work.

Convy was one of those performers who was never in the regular cast of a successful or long-running series but somehow would always end up as TV's go-to guy, whether it was as a guest star (i.e., pretty much every third episode of *The Love Boat*) or a celebrity panelist on a game show.

I auditioned and won the chance to do *Craziest Things* as one of the people who would set up the stunts on camera. I ended up as pretty much the "main guy" because of either my fearless nature or my cavalier attitude (or a little of each). I ultimately shot about a dozen segments for the show (not all of which aired).

As tried-and-true as the hidden camera formula should've proven, the producers added several unique elements that had everyone—including those of us working there—trying to figure out just what in the world they were thinking. It was nothing outrageous. Quite the contrary: just lame.

One example: we would bring a psychologist in and while the segments were on Convy would discuss with them some of the behavioral reasons that our "marks" were reacting the way they were to what we had set up. This was probably interesting on some level, but trying to make the show "educational" in some way was just one of many miscalculations.

Though we were trying to use the element of surprise, during at least one segment in which I starred the surprise ended up being on us. The set-up was this: I would be standing on a busy street in front of an office building. I was wearing a suit, but my shirt had a very noticeable grape juice stain on it.

I would tell passers-by that I was in a predicament—on my way to a short but crucial interview and had just spilled the juice on myself—and asked if I could borrow their shirt. I told them I would only be a few minutes, after which I would come right back out and return it.

After a segment with Zsa Zsa or Eva Gabor . . . it's one or the other

The other Gabor, I guess

9:30 7 3 PEOPLE DO THE CRAZIEST THINGS (CC)
Passersby help scare Bob Perlow out of the hiccups; motorists are asked to give a ride to a hitchhiking orangutan; Steve Bond of "General Hospital" surprises a woman doing a soap-opera scene with her husband.
HBO MOVIE—Adventure; 1 hr., 45 min.
"Conan the Destroyer."
[Closed-captioned.]
LIF FAMILY GUIDE PRESENTS—Magazine
USA NIGHT FLIGHT
Scenes from new movies including "Day of the Dead," "Silverado" and "Pale Rider."

July 19 1985

A programming guide from July 19, 1985, advertises the night's episode of People Do the Craziest Things

men would give me for not being able or willing to (literally) give me their shirt off their back. Yet *every single person* I asked was happy to remove his shirt and loan it to me for my "interview!" We were astounded . . . I mean, who, even to this day, would do that for someone they'd just met?

Still, as soon as the show began airing, it would be us—and the network—who ended up losing our shirt. *Craziest Things* premiered on Thursday, September 20, 1984. We were up against *Magnum, P. I.*, a top ten show, which we assumed was going to be our biggest hurdle. Little did we know.

This scheduling also put us directly up against the premier of a new series called *The Cosby Show*. But we weren't too worried about that one, since sitcoms had declined in popularity over the past few years. We figured that we were in a position to at least make a decent showing.

We didn't. Not by any single definition of the term "decent showing."

Most people agree that if you're going to get bad news, it's best to get it as fast as possible. Well, at least *that* happened:

the A. C. Neilson Company has something called "overnight ratings" (or simply "overnights"), which are just what they sound like. This may be one of the few truly kind aspects of the television industry—you really don't spend a lot of time worrying whether or not you're screwed.

That Friday morning, we saw our ratings. We didn't simply lose the timeslot. We got killed. *Annihilated.* My initial thought was that it's a really, really good thing I didn't quit any of my regular warmup gigs in favor of doing this show. Bambi had fared better, as Godzilla—or Cosby, as some called him—not only won the timeslot but ended up as the highest-rated show of the week (and subsequently the whole season and the remainder of the Eighties).

The following Thursday at 8:00 p.m. our second episode ran, and for this airing the ratings wouldn't be as bad. They were *worse.* (Even I watched *Cosby* that night.) This time we were up against a *Cosby* episode where the family holds a bathroom funeral for a pet goldfish. I still get misty thinking about it . . . primarily for what it did to *my* show. We ended up getting flushed right alongside the tiny gilled corpse: ABC cancelled *People Do the Craziest Things* immediately after that second outing.

Ironically, under different circumstances they might have kept us on. In some cases, networks go through "let's keep it on and see what happens" cycles. But moreover, once the networks started realizing that pretty much anything opposite *Cosby* was going to get destroyed, they began simply scheduling sacrificial lambs against it, shows like *Ripley's Believe It or Not* and *Our World* that were less expensive to produce (so it didn't matter as much that so few people watched).

Our show could've been one of them, since our production costs were also very much on the low end. But back in the fall of 1984 ABC was still looking for something that had a chance of holding its own against *Cosby*, and *Craziest Things* just wasn't going to cut it. Several of the remaining episodes ended up airing in random timeslots, but that was the end of the line.

It's safe to say that *People Do the Craziest Things* has pretty much been forgotten. As of 2015 the show doesn't even have a Wikipedia page dedicated to it. Imdb.com, on the other hand, simply dismisses it as a "somewhat mean-spirited takeoff on *Candid Camera.*" *Ouch.* (Perhaps accurate, but *ouch* nevertheless.)

Still, if there was a silver lining, it's that sitcoms had been said to be in a recession during the early Eighties, a situation changed overnight by *The Cosby Show*, which in turn ended up helping my "real" career doing audience warmup. *People Do the Craziest Things* may have been a failure, but it was fun. A fun failure. And that's the only way to fail.

Chapter Twelve

Night of the Comet

Very, very few people have seen a 1980 movie in which I had a small role called *Stunt Rock*, so if purely by default my only notable appearance in a feature film was in *Night of the Comet*, a horror comedy released in 1984. Early that year a friend had introduced me to a woman who turned out to be a Hollywood casting agent. Three weeks later, she called and asked if I wanted to read for a small part in the film.

In the movie, a comet is scheduled to fly past the earth, which everyone looks forward to watching. But the joke's on you, earthlings! As soon as the comet passes, it does almost no physical damage but instantly vaporizes nearly the entire human race, except for a handful who happened to have been holed up in structures that shielded them from the rays. A few other people who had been spared from the vaporization get turned into zombies. (Bear in mind that at no point did anyone claim this movie was *The Godfather*.)

I appear about six minutes into the movie for less than thirty seconds. So if reading this has compelled you to go stream *Night of the Comet*, you can stop watching after that point. (Just kidding. Please watch the whole thing. I get about nine cents every time it's shown.) I play a television reporter. There are only two shots of me, and in both of them I appear on a TV screen. Yes, even doing a feature film, I *still* couldn't get away from television.

I only filmed for a couple of hours. It was a location shoot, on Vine Street in Los Angeles in front of the famous Capital Records building (although you can't see it in the shot).

In the film, I appear to be looking at news copy, so if you

watch it you might assume I'm reading my lines. I'm actually not reading lines since I didn't have any: they knew that I was an improv comic and not really an "actor," so I was told to ad-lib the scene (*that* I could do), and try it about four different ways. They ended up using a take highlighted by my character being unsure just how to pronounce "Newfoundland."

While I'm still speaking, lying on the sofa in her living room, a very Eighties-looking character—a girl with big hair, wearing spandex and leg-warmers (think Jane Fonda workout video)—picks up a remote control, aims it at the TV, and *click!* That's it for me, at least in terms of this particular movie. The comet hits about five minutes later, and presumably my character gets vaporized along with everyone else.

Although *Night of the Comet* did okay at the box office (it made four times its budget) and would go on to develop a healthy cult following, I've honestly never been approached or contacted by anyone asking about the movie. (I appear six minutes in, so I guess people maybe weren't done buying popcorn while I was onscreen.) Still, it's ironic that my most enduring on-camera appearance would be a movie about the end of the world.

And even though I only worked on the movie for about the length of time it takes to watch it, *Night of the Comet* would come to have special meaning to me. Case in point: a few years later I tracked down and bought a copy of the movie poster. This was pre-internet and pre-eBay, so finding it took some doing; I had to contact one of those poster and memorabilia specialty shops and ended up paying probably way too much. Nonetheless, the poster adorns my living room wall to this day.

Chapter Thirteen

Growing Pains

It seems like the ultimate public relations cliché whenever anyone states that the cast of a show *about* a family becomes *like* a family. But from what I observed, at least, it's an apt description in terms of one of the most successful shows I ever did: *Growing Pains*. I was fortunate enough to become part of the show's extended family, and I would become especially close to the star, Alan Thicke.

Thicke was coming off a series of personal and professional setbacks in the mid-Eighties, the epicenter of which was his late night talk show, *Thicke of the Night*. Although the show's emphasis on comedy made it probably a bit more comparable to the still-on-the-rise David Letterman, Thicke's syndicated entry was on directly against *The Tonight Show Starring Johnny Carson* in most markets.

Despite how long Carson had been on by that point, *The Tonight Show* was still a ratings behemoth and considered synonymous with late-night TV. Thicke was an unknown, at least outside of his native Canada, so the notion that he could even challenge Carson, let alone best him, was met with derision. Thicke's ratings were accordingly weak, and the show was cancelled after less than a year.

Even though statistically speaking more TV shows fail than succeed, the press was particularly harsh towards *Thicke of the Night*. They painted it as the *Heaven's Gate* of TV, or at least talk shows, for pretty much no good reason other than that the host had a funny-sounding name that easily lent itself to bad puns (which even he pretty much acknowledged via the show's title).

In the very definition of adding insult to injury, his show had been cancelled on the same day that Thicke was served divorce papers by his first wife, the musician and former soap opera actress Gloria Loring. Thicke has told me that he went into a deep depression during this period, concerned that the only other thing he might be qualified to do was drive a Zamboni (a career path that probably all hockey-playing Canadians contemplate as some point).

Growing Pains would come along just in time to keep him off the Zamboni (or worse). Thicke's acting experience was minimal beyond a supporting role in a made-for-TV movie called *Calendar Girl Murders*. (Remember watching that one? No? Neither does he.) But something about Thicke strongly suggested that he might make a good TV father— maybe even a *quintessential* TV father (a la Robert Young)—

Bob with Alan Thicke

as he had all the qualities they were looking for: handsome, smart, and funny.

Thicke was the father of two sons in real life (from his first marriage), both of whom would have a regular presence at the *Growing Pains* tapings. His younger son Robin was about seven when the show began, and it was not unusual to see the little brat running up and down the bleachers while I was trying to do the warmup.

Of course, I couldn't really do or say anything since he was the star's son, so I basically just put up with it. Today, as most everyone knows, Robin Thicke is a multi-platinum-selling recording artist. He's also a very nice and well-adjusted individual (so clearly he didn't suffer from any sort of lack of discipline as a child).

I was doing warmup for the show since the pilot, and Alan Thicke and I had quickly become friends. It was nothing beyond the simple fact that we were about the same age and both single at the time. Not merely single, but *show biz* single, which is a whole other world (a fun, whirlwind of a world).

Thicke would often invite a beautiful girl to the tapings (sometimes more than one at a time, even three). Then during one of the breaks, he would call me over, direct my attention to his female guest(s) and ask, "What do you think?" He didn't actually need my opinion; he knew perfectly well they were all hot.

I would spend a lot of time with Thicke outside of the tapings as well. As he was between marriages, I would often be his "plus one" for whatever guest list he happened to be on (and that was most of them). Once we arrived at our destination, we would usually look for (more) women, almost inevitably with success (at least for him—wingmen frequently end up outside the plane trying to get in, like in that famous *Twilight Zone* episode starring another Canadian, William Shatner).

We went to a lot of live entertainment events together, and I would also end up acting as his "front." I would go to the backstage door and tell the guy that Alan Thicke was here and wanted to come meet Wayne Newton or George

Carlin or whomever we were seeing on any given night. I may have been mistaken once or twice for being Thicke's personal assistant, but that was nothing that ever bothered me. If anything I liked it, being famous by association.

One of our most unusual encounters would have to have been the one with Sam Kinison, the brash, loud, dirty (better make that very brash, very loud, and very dirty . . . and very brilliant) stand-up comic who would end up being killed in an auto accident in 1992. While we were all hanging out in his dressing room, Kinison said something about how crazy it was that America's dad would be friends with America's worst nightmare.

Around 1988, another thing happened that could have been a story right out of the sitcom. Hockey superstar Wayne Gretzky had shaken the entire NHL up when it was announced that he was being traded by the Edmonton Oilers to the LA Kings. This was because the Canadian fans deeply resented one of

Bob with Wayne Gretsky

their own going over to a US team, especially the greatest hockey player ever. (They were willing to give up Thicke, but never Gretzky.)

Thicke, who had been friends with the athlete for many years, allowed Gretzky to quite literally hide out at his house in Toluca Lake until the story had blown over in the sports press. Although I knew that Gretzky was there, I was sworn to absolute secrecy, to which I of course complied. (I suppose it's okay to spill the beans *now* because obviously he's not there anymore.)

On the subject of sports, one year I accompanied Thicke to Hawaii for the Marjoe Gortner Tennis Tournament. This was a charity event paid for by sponsorship where hundreds of celebrities would gather and play tennis and golf for a good cause.

One afternoon we were attending the tennis matches. These weren't formal "games" so much as stars volleying back and forth with other stars until they felt like vacating the place to someone else. When we got there, doubles play was underway.

One of the four people playing was Chevy Chase. Chase, of course, was best known for being the first breakout performer of *Saturday Night Live* back in 1975 and the star of the *National Lampoon's Vacation* movie series. At the moment he was playing alongside Carl Weathers, who portrayed Apollo Creed in the *Rocky* movies (at least until Dolph Lundgren kills him in the fourth one).

Chase announced that he was "a bit tired" and asked for someone to step in for him. I volunteered and came down to the court, racket in hand. After I looked across the court to see whom I was playing against, I said derisively, "Hey, wait—I'm not playing against some *chick*!"

The entire crowd gasped, naturally, at my apparently sexist, crude comment, until they saw who it was I had just called "some chick": Chris Evert, who everyone knew was one of the greatest tennis players of all time. (She also happened to be one of the nicest.) As soon as everyone realized I was being ironic, the crowd broke into hysterical laughter.

Just like that, out of the corner of my eye, I could see Chase. He had already packed up his tennis gear and put his jacket on, but as soon as he heard all the laughs that my spur-of-the-moment quip had gotten, he decided to do a 180-degree turn. He claimed he had gotten his "second wind" and demanded to reclaim the position on the court that he had just vacated to me.

Even though I was glad to get one big laugh in and have

Bob with Chevy Chase

Bob with Chris Evert

them asking, "Who was that guy?" decades later the whole Chevy Chase thing still riles me. First of all, this was a charity event, and everyone was supposed to have left their egos in the locker rooms. I barely qualify as a "celebrity," at least within that crowd, and yet someone at Chase's career-level at the time apparently is so desperate to be the center of attention he wouldn't even allow a non-celebrity like me to get a single, spontaneous laugh in.

Okay, so, with *that* off my chest . . .

Another favorite destination that Thicke and I would frequent was the Playboy Mansion in Holmby Hills, California. Some would argue that the *Playboy* lifestyle—the magazine and the lush private residence—had lost its relevance by the Reagan years, either because AIDS had made sexual promiscuity a thing of the past or conversely because magazines like *Hustler* had made Hugh Hefner's world seem pedestrian.

Bob inside the Playboy Mansion

Well, if you're of a certain age growing up with the aura of *Playboy*, or even if you had simply visited the mansion during the Eighties, you certainly wouldn't say that. First of all, we had to go through five—count 'em, *five*—checkpoints just to get to the front door. The White House is probably easier get to into (though with good reason: the Mansion's a *lot* more fun).

Once inside the mansion, you would see every famous actor and sports figure you could think of, and as you would imagine, every girl there was beautiful. This was far from a happy coincidence: each one who was not already firmly ensconced in the *Playboy* empire in some way was at least *trying* to be.

All of these girls had to submit a professional headshot—that was essentially their "audition"—which sometimes only got them as far as these parties (which for most of them, sad to say, would end up being the extent of their association with *Playboy* or even show business in general; this may seem humiliating, but it was Hollywood).

Lest it sound like I'm suggesting that Alan Thicke was some kind of womanizer (even if I was engaging in the exact same activities myself), I should point out that I was in the wedding party when he remarried in 1994 to former Miss World Gina Tolleson. The marriage only lasted about five years but produced Thicke's beloved third son, Carter.

With all this extracurricular activity, somehow Alan Thicke and I both found time to work on *Growing Pains*. The show was more than just a hit: it represented the silencing of his small army of detractors who had gathered after his talk show bombed. Critics had stopped hating on Thicke personally only to move onto accusing the show of ripping off *Family Ties*.

At the time I stopped doing the show regularly, after the third season, Kirk Cameron was moving towards his now-well-known religious persuasion. Although he was not as overtly Christian as he would be later on after the show ended, little by little he would start to make demands regarding some of the content of the scripts that he found objectionable based on his faith.

While I was there, however, Cameron had another personal interest, and this one I had a bit of a problem with: he kept pet snakes and would have them in the studio, walking around with those slithery little SOBs around his neck. I don't have ophidiophobia (the irrational fear of snakes) *per se*, but there's just something about people "wearing" pets as accessories—whether it's snakes, parrots, or iguanas—that I find creepy, the same way I find mimes, jugglers, and clowns creepy. (So I suppose if I ever come across a juggling mime wearing a red nose with a snake around his neck, I'm outta here.)

After I stopped doing the warmup at the end of the third season I assumed that I was done with the show. However, since I had been there at the beginning, they asked me to come back for the final episode as sort of a representation of the whole thing coming full circle. I was flown in as a surprise for the cast for what would be a very fun reunion and a nice gesture for a deserving group of people.

Bob with Kirk Cameron

Bob with Joanna Kerns

Meanwhile, I'm just so happy that my pal Alan Thicke finally found the happiness he truly deserves when he married the love of his life, Tanya Callau, in 2005. At the same time, there's clearly no keeping him off TV: in 2014 he, his wife, and son Carter began starring in a successful mock-reality show called *Unusually Thicke*. More importantly, he and I remain close friends.

Chapter Fourteen

Full House

My connection to *Full House* went a little beyond simply being "hired" to do the audience warmup. I had been close friends with the creator of the show, Jeff Franklin, since he and I started out together as apprentice writers on *Laverne & Shirley* in 1978.

After that show ended in 1983, Franklin ended up as a writer on one of the most innovative sitcoms on TV at the time (*It's Garry Shandling's Show*), but he also wanted to do his own series and spent several years pitching various ideas. Nearly all his efforts initially failed; most of the time when he suggested a concept, he'd typically be told that the network already had something similar in the pipeline.

In 1987 Franklin finally hit pay dirt . . . without trying to. In fact, at that point he was attempting just the opposite. He was looking for a way to get bought out of a deal he was in with a production company, so he pitched "the lamest concept he could think of." Instead of offering him a settlement and sending him on his way, which he had been hoping, they bought the idea.

Franklin's "lame" but surprisingly lucrative pitch was a show about three single men living together raising children. It probably didn't hurt that a very similar concept had been a hugely successful movie just a couple of years earlier, *Three Men and a Baby*. And no, I don't know what became of Steve Gutenberg.

Once fleshed out, the premise ended up with the three men being a widowed father, his late wife's younger brother, and the father's best friend from childhood. Stand-up comic Bob

Saget was Franklin's first choice for the role of the father, Danny Tanner. But while the original pilot was being shot, Saget was under contract with CBS (doing the comic relief on *CBS This Morning*) and temporarily unavailable. The part ended up being played—for the first and only time—by John Posey. (Posey would never have much success, but his son Tyler would become relatively popular as the star of the MTV series *Teen Wolf* in the 2010s.)

Saget did become available after the show was picked up, which was good news for everyone (except John Posey). Saget, interestingly, had also done time down in the trenches—or rather up in the bleachers—as a warmup comic. In fact, a few years earlier I would sub for him occasionally while he had been the regular warmup on *Bosom Buddies*.

The only thing that could have made Saget seem like an odd choice for *Full House* was the fact that he did—and continues to do—a stand-up act loaded with sexual content and extremely blatant profanity. Some parents would later even suggest that Saget had been luring an inappropriate audience towards his filthy material using two family shows—this one and *America's Funniest Home Videos*, which he hosted from 1989 to 1997—as a Trojan horse.

There was actually no such sublimation going on: Saget always kept his two careers entirely separate. He never had any contempt for doing wholesome material, and he loved being America's favorite TV dad. (Not only was he a dad in real life but his children consisted of three daughters, just as they would on the show.)

Dave Coulier was cast as Danny's best friend, Joey Gladstone. In sharp contrast to Saget, Coulier was a family-friendly stand-up comic as well as a cartoon voice artist, and both of these traits would be used for the character.

One idiosyncrasy of Coulier's that was not transferred to his character—thankfully—was that the actor had a constant problem with flatulence. If you watch the reruns, in scenes with Coulier you can sometimes see the other performers appear to be gingerly stepping out of fallout area.

Bob with Lori Loughlin and Dave Coulier

Bob with John Stamos

The only "name" attached to the show when it began was John Stamos, who played Danny's brother-in-law Jesse Katsopolis. The character's last name had been "Cochran" during the first season, but Stamos requested that it be changed. No, not because of Johnny Cochran, but in order to reflect his own Greek heritage. The character's fixation with Elvis Presley, however, came from an appreciation for the King that Stamos, but especially Franklin, shared.

Stamos had begun appearing on *General Hospital* in early 1982, playing a character with the type of name that only exists on soap operas ("Blackie Parrish." *Seriously.*) He had only been part of that ensemble cast for a little over two years, but that was enough for him to become a minor TV teen idol.

Prime time would not be imminently cordial to John Stamos. In the fall of 1984, two major network shows inspired by MTV music videos premiered. Unfortunately, rather than *Miami Vice*, Stamos got the one that was not a hit—*Dreams*. He didn't have much more luck with his next sitcom, *You Again?*, even with the great Jack Klugman as his costar.

Despite the setbacks, Stamos not only fit right in with *Full House* but his still-in-effect popularity helped give the show a boost when it started out. The Jesse character loved his three nieces but had some trouble leaving his rebellious streak behind him, which sometimes put him at odds with his brother-in-law Danny.

This friction carried over into real life: Stamos and Saget did not get along for the first year and a half of the show, although they would eventually end up being very close friends and remain so to this day.

Eldest daughter D.J. (Donna Jo) Tanner was played by Candace Cameron (who now goes by her married name, Candace Cameron Bure, after marrying Russian hockey star Valeri Bure in 1996). Candace was the younger sister of *Growing Pains* star/teen idol Kirk Cameron, who appears on a first-season episode of *Full House* as her cousin.

Five-year-old Jodie Sweetin was cast as middle daughter Stephanie. Sweetin's experience at the time was limited to an

Oscar Meyer commercial and an appearance on the show *Valerie*, but you would never know this from the way she always knew all her lines by heart. She usually knew *the whole script* by heart. Sweetin was one sharp little girl.

Youngest daughter Michelle was written as an infant when the show began. California law limits the number of hours per week that a child under age five can work, which necessitated that Michelle—like nearly all characters that age—be played by twins. This casting is usually fairly random,

Bob with Mary Kate and Ashley Olsen

involving little requirement beyond being cute and having parents willing to put them on TV.

The twins found to play baby Michelle would be Mary-Kate and Ashley Olsen. It's become customary for sitcom babies to skip a few years so that after a season or two they end up being recast as a five-year-old. However, producers of *Full House* took the somewhat unusual step of allowing Michelle to age in real time and kept the twins sharing the role until age eight. They just suspected, quite accurately, that the Olsens were something special.

As popular as the girls would become, there's a reason so few sitcoms use children who fall within that age where they're too old to be pretty much just "carried around" but still too small to be counted on for full cooperation. So using the Olsen twins at that in-between age did cause problems, or at the very least complications. Once they were old enough to talk, most of their lines had to be fed to them from offstage by a professional children's acting coach.

Sometimes getting just a *shot* of either Mary-Kate or Ashley would be time-consuming. When Michelle would give the thumbs-up and say in her angelic little voice, "You got it, *dude*!" hearts melted all over America. It was a bit of a different story in the studio, when getting this shot with her saying the line exactly right could take up to twenty minutes or more.

The reason this would take so long was usually not because the girls were unable to say the line. Kids, in fact, are natural mimics. The main problem was usually getting them to say the line while they looked at the character in the show that they were supposed to be addressing, rather than looking at their coach or one of their parents, if they were on set.

If you watch carefully, you'll notice that it's usually the same case with dogs on TV and in the movies. *Full House* had its own resident pooch, a golden retriever named Comet. In real life, Jeff Franklin is a big fan of that breed. It's not hard to catch the dog glancing offstage, because that's where his trainer would be.

Everyone knows the old show business saying that advises actors to avoid working with children and animals. Although this adage traditionally refers to the adults risking being upstaged, another problem is that using kids and dogs does slow the whole process down considerably.

Comet, whose real name was Buddy, would go on to star (yes, star) in a successful (yes, successful) feature film, *Air Bud,* in 1997 (yes, '97). Of course, this was *still* a dog's life compared to what the Olson twins managed to pull off. For Mary-Kate and Ashley, *Full House* would end up as merely a springboard.

During the remainder of their childhood, the two created a brand name through a series of home videos, clothing, and other merchandise, practically inventing the market aimed specifically at six-to-twelve-year-olds. Their collective worth today is said to be—are you sitting down?—a billion dollars. Which leads the rest of us to wonder exactly what we're doing wrong. *I* can say "You got it, dude!" while looking at another character, and *I'm* not a billionaire.

Even before the Olsens became a marketing phenomenon independent of *Full House,* they, along with the other two girls, were a big part of why kids watched the show. Because of this, the producers decided to forgo the standard age minimum of sixteen for attendance to a live taping, lowering it to ten (provided, of course, that they were accompanied by an adult).

Whenever I, or other people who do audience warmup, am asked to describe the job, the most common answer is usually, "It's like being a substitute teacher." More aptly, it's like being a babysitter. So with all the kids we had in the audience for *Full House* (even though they came with adult supervision), those descriptions were never closer to being accurate. With any luck I was a *funny* babysitter, but a babysitter nonetheless.

I did most of the *Full House* tapings over the show's eight-year run (as well as writing two episodes, acting in three, and helping to punch up scripts as needed). Another analogy would be that it was basically like working a kid's birthday party; why I didn't end up being required to wear a red clown nose I still haven't figured out, but to this day I am thankful. But I would do a lot of my usual warmup activities, like games and sing-alongs.

I also stuck with my standard procedure of giving away t-shirts. This would rarely fail to pacify audience members, the small ones as well as the X-large. The one thing I still refrained from giving out, however, was candy. Earlier I explained the rush-then-crash dynamic that makes candy for a studio audience a bad idea. Well, it's an even worse idea for an audience full of kids.

Thankfully I was never dealing with very small children, and those who were in attendance were usually so excited to see the stars of the show (particularly the Olsen twins and the other kids) and have the chance to watch the show being taped that for the most part they behaved themselves. (Although I stress "for the *most* part.")

Finding kid-appropriate ways to keep the crowd occupied during what was usually a four- to five-hour taping was sometimes a challenge. For some reason, lip-syncing seems to be a hit with all ages. I would often do Creedence Clearwater Revival's "Bad Moon Rising"—mainly because it's a very easy song to lip-sync to—and one time even got to do it when John Fogerty, the song's writer and original singer, who was attending the taping with his stepdaughter Lyndsey, was in the audience. My rendition got an approving nod and smile from him.

Fogerty wasn't the only classic rocker to drop in on the *House*: the Beach Boys—including reclusive founding member/songwriter Brian Wilson—appeared on the show in the second season. The group at the time was enjoying the success of a number one single, "Kokomo." It was Stamos, a huge fan and occasional *member*, who got them on the show.

There must have been something about *Full House* that attracted pre-Beatles pop icons who were in the midst of a comeback: Frankie Avalon and Annette Funicello, the royal couple of Sixties beach movies, appeared as themselves in 1991. Both of them were incredibly nice, particularly a relief since, as mentioned earlier, Annette had been my boyhood crush.

The two had recently had a successful reunion movie (*Back to the Beach*), but sadly their renewed success now had limitations because of Annette's multiple sclerosis. But this episode also snuck in a third guest star playing himself. In case you haven't seen it—no, it wasn't Sean Connery. Nope, not Barry Williams from *The Brady Bunch* either. Keep guessing.

Give up? Okay—it was *me*, yours truly, Bob Perlow. The episode involved Joey shooting a sitcom pilot with the two guests, and in one scene I appear doing the audience warmup. I was shot with a hand-held camera among the real bleachers and actual studio audience used for the show. The credit even read "Bob Perlow as Himself" (which undoubtedly had the entire nation asking the question: *Who?*).

That same season ended with the revelation that the character Rebecca (Lori Loughlin) was pregnant. Loughlin had joined the cast several seasons earlier as a love interest for Jesse, and the characters were married not long after. Unfortunately, behind the scenes we all realized exactly what a fictitious TV baby meant: that the show was now officially running on empty. And the "baby" ended up being twins, so you do the math.

At the end of the 1992 season, ratings were still solid but ABC decided that the cost of production was simply too high to keep the show on the air. Contrary to what was reported at the time—that the show was canceled during a hiatus—we did shoot the final episode with the realization that it was, well, the final episode (in which Michelle falls off a horse and gets amnesia; so we didn't jump the shark so much as we were eaten by it).

There was talk that the show would move over to the WB, one of two new broadcast networks, along with UPN, launched in the mid-Nineties. The two merged to form the CW in 2008. However, Stamos did not want to continue the show on an upstart network, feeling like it would be too much of a step down.

Still, this was not to be the end for *Full House*, not by a long shot. Even though it may not have been as successful in its original run as, say, *Cheers*, *Full House* is the type of show that in the business is called "evergreen." Since the show is aimed mainly at kids, its audience will regenerate every five years or so, with fresh viewers for whom the show is "new." So in turn the property will always end up generating a considerable amount of income (hence, ever*green*).

This may well change at some point, as some of the technology that has emerged in the time since the sitcom aired becomes conspicuous in its absence: kids may start to wonder why there are no cellphones or references to the Internet or social networking and therefore may not be able to relate to the show as much.

For the time being, however, *Full House* is probably safe. The show, a concept originally designed as self-sabotage like in *The Producers*, has already done quite well for my old buddy Jeff Franklin, who as a result of its success now lives in an nine bedroom/eighteen bathroom mansion in Beverly Hills. (An interesting sidenote: the house that had previously stood on the grounds had been demolished. No, not because it was old or in any way unsafe . . . but because it had been the site of the notorious murder of Sharon Tate by Charles Manson's cohorts in 1969.)

An X-rated comedian, another who couldn't control his farts, babies with a net worth exceeding that of some small countries, and now a connection to the Sharon Tate murders?

Have no fear. It's going to take a lot more than all that to undo the purity—spirit *and* execution—of *Full House*. Even with the tension between Stamos and Saget during the first few years (long since resolved), everyone seemed to get along for the most part. I witnessed few if any tantrums or arguments. There was hugging on camera, and there was hugging off-camera (unless Coulier farted). These were all people who were glad to be working together.

The cast and crew of Full House, 1991

That said, had I not been involved with it, *Full House* is probably not a show I myself would have ever watched—not even when I was a kid. But I'm not the audience they were going for, which clearly they had no trouble finding. So it's win-win. In 2015 it was even announced that there would be a follow-up series, *Fuller House*. But the original series obviously made—and continues to makes—a lot of people happy, and who wouldn't want to be a part of that?

Chapter Fifteen

Who's the Boss?

The sport of boxing has often been used as an analogy for starting from nothing and rising to the top, perhaps most successfully by Sylvester Stallone in *Rocky* (including all thirty-seven sequels . . . right up to the one where his fight is with the nurses at the assisted living facility trying to wipe the drool off his chin).

Tony Danza had been a professional boxer before becoming an actor, which is fitting when you look at his career. In 1978 he had been cast on *Taxi* almost entirely for type, since he would be playing a prize fighter. Sure, he was also handsome and charismatic, but strictly speaking he wasn't an actor.

Concerned that the inexperienced Danza might not recognize his cues, the producers changed the character's name from "Phil" to "Tony" just days before the filming was to begin. Not wanting to insult Danza or undermine his confidence, the producers withheld the truth from him, telling him instead that they were giving the character his own name because of the fondness they'd developed for him. Danza went along with it willingly, but he has said that he was perfectly aware all along of what was really going on.

So even back then, Tony Danza knew a lot more than anyone was willing to give him credit for. It turns out he wasn't merely smart—he was *very* smart.

One only needs to look at *Who's the Boss?* to understand how far Tony Danza had come from that early experience: in the course of a single show, he would go from being treated like he needed his hand held to ruling with an iron fist. Danza was not simply the star of *Who's the Boss?*—he pretty much was the show. This is what I found out when I worked there as a writer for two years starting in 1988.

I was now about a decade into doing audience warmup, and my writing partner, Gene Braunstein, and I had spent a couple of seasons as story editors on *She's the Sheriff*. (That show's star, Suzanne Somers, was far and away one of the nicest people we've ever worked with.) The day-to-day experience was extremely positive, but we were airing in first-run syndication, generally the TV equivalent of the minor leagues. Plus we knew in our hearts that it really wasn't a very good show, as much as we loved the environment.

Looking to move a bit up the ladder, we decided we would pursue positions on *Who's the Boss?*, a top ten show on ABC. It had a unique if not entirely plausible premise. Danza played Tony Micelli, an ex-pro baseball player (maybe making him a boxer again might have been too predictable). Micelli was a widower who decided he didn't want to raise his young daughter, Samantha (Alyssa Milano), in the city.

Micelli takes a position in suburban Connecticut as a housekeeper for a female advertising executive, Angela Bower (Judith Light), who was in the process of getting divorced and had a young son (Danny Pintauro). Tony and Samantha move into the house, which by one of those astonishing sitcom coincidences just happened to have enough spare bedrooms for everyone.

The show premiered as one of the new crop of fall shows in 1984 and was originally scheduled Thursday nights at 8:30 on ABC. What no one expected, however, was that Hurricane Cosby would sweep through the fall schedule, with Thursday nights as the eye of the storm.

The Cosby Show shot right to number one, taking *Family Ties*, which was up against *Who's the Boss?*, up with it. *Boss* had a lead-in that turned out to be not quite as reliable: *People Do the Craziest Things*, a show that I just happened to be on (as explained in a previous chapter).

In response to the situation, the alphabet network had to jettison one of the two shows and decided to save *Who's*

Bob with Suzanne Somers

the Boss? rather than mine. So I suppose it's either irony or karma that I ended up working on *Boss* (which was moved to Tuesday nights, where it gradually ended up beating *The A-Team*).

The producers of *Who's the Boss?* would explain the show's somewhat ambiguous title by saying that in some episodes Angela was "the boss," in other episodes it was Tony, and in still others it would be Angela's mother, Mona, played by Katherine Helmond. Viewers, then, would have the fun of figuring it out for themselves.

But as soon as Geno and I got hired for the writing staff in 1987, it didn't take us long to figure out that behind the scenes the show's title was purely rhetorical, and no such round robin was being played with the authority. Who was the boss? Tony Danza was the boss, there was absolutely no question.

Although Danza had no kind of credit as a producer on the sitcom, it was very clear on the set that everyone had to answer to him. Working with him could be a mixed blessing, and possibly no one was more aware of that than he was.

There was one particular week that will live in infamy, at least among people who worked on the show. Danza was just completely unhappy with the script and spent the entire period from when it was submitted up to and including the taping just screaming violently at everyone in sight. The ordeal ended, however, the following Monday when he came into the studio with t-shirts for everyone that read "I SURVIVED SHOW '7,'" the "7" referring to the show that we had done that week. (Ah, t-shirts, friend and foe through my entire career.)

Or something like that. I actually don't remember the exact words on the shirt, and when I recently contacted one of the show's producers, he didn't remember either. (Maybe neither of us wanted to look back at it and laugh as much as we wanted to simply forget it. It was rough, no question.) But this does just illustrate that Tony Danza, for all his talent and commitment, often did run hot and cold.

Some of the other cast members had their own methods for keeping the writers on our toes. Although Helmond had an extensive résumé doing all types of roles, including drama, she was best known for her role as Jessica Tate on the farcical sitcom *Soap* and thus was generally thought of more as a comedienne.

Ergo, we were a bit surprised and confused by the manner in which she would often conduct herself at the table read: the way she would rarely smile or make jokes, you'd think we were reading a will, not a comedy script. We all worried, thinking that this somehow indicated she was unhappy with what we had come up with, but it would always turn out she was only saving her comedic energy for the tapings, when as Mona she would cut loose and have everyone rolling in the aisles.

Although the producers knew about my professional warmup credentials, I was informed they did not want me to do it for *Boss*. They told me that since I was a member of the writing staff, they didn't want my attention divided. (I also didn't do the warmup for other shows during this period.) I was actually flattered: they were indicating clearly that I had value as a writer when I was already well established doing warmup.

About which, Danza was perhaps most authoritative when the show was actually taping in front of the studio audience. Once they were done filming a scene, it was Danza who would usually decree, "Okay, let's move on!" which indicated that everyone was done with that scene. Danza rarely waited to find out whether or not the director agreed (or cared if he did), which in turn kept them from being able to shoot the endless retakes that were endemic in the sitcom world.

Danza was able to do this because none of the directors or producers ever wanted to argue with him. It wasn't because he was a boxer, or even because he could have a temper. It was actually something quite a bit more civilized, though no less intimidating: they were all too aware that he was in a position to have them, let's just say, "not rehired."

But I believe it was just as well. The way I'm describing things it might sound like Danza was looking to cut corners, or even was lazy, or didn't respect the authority of people who were there to do a specific job. However, as someone who's been present at as many tapings as I have, I can safely say that the majority of the time when Danza made the decision that what they'd shot was "good enough," *he was right.*

Most sitcoms that use a studio audience will do reshoots even if they already had one take that went perfectly (and may well end up being the one used for the final edit). This isn't wrong so much as it's superfluous. Danza knew perfectly well that a single "good" take should do the job (say nothing of the fact that comedy, by definition, is supposed to have a level of spontaneity to it). The audience, by their laughs, would be an indication.

If you watch old reruns of *I Love Lucy* and *The Honeymooners*, you might notice that in some episodes there are mistakes. Not look-carefully-did-you-catch-that mistakes, but conspicuous and obvious ones. This is because those shows very rarely, if ever, did retakes and typically only stopped filming when it was absolutely necessary, usually just to change the scenery.

Because of the no-nonsense approach that Danza, essentially, forced on everyone else, *Who's the Boss?* ended up having the tightest tapings of any sitcom I was ever involved with, usually lasting only a little over two hours. So when the show aired, most of the time you knew you were listening to the genuine, spontaneous laughter of the crowd. It made a difference.

However, on one episode it had become necessary to use a laugh track, since we weren't able to use a studio audience at all. But it's safe to say it was a fair trade-off. Unlike the aforementioned *I Love Lucy*, *Who's the Boss?* did not make a lot of use of celebrities coming on the show as themselves; our show's premise arguably didn't support that. But one of the few times we did go that route, we pulled out all the stops.

In one of his only sitcom appearances ever, Frank Sinatra

agreed to do the show in 1989. However, for security reasons, he did not want to do the show with the live audience. Everyone on staff may have known not to cross Danza, but Danza in turn knew enough not to argue with The Chairman of the Board. So we set up a special taping to accommodate Sinatra, not even doing it on our usually scheduled day.

While heading towards the end of my second season on the show, I got a call from my agent. (Yes, I had an agent. I was very much now in show business.) He told me that NBC was putting together a new show, *House Party* hosted by Washington TV correspondent Steve Doocy (much more on him later), and they wanted to create an on-air segment around me.

I immediately decided I wanted to accept the offer, which was going to mean relocating to New York City. Even after the debacle of *People Do the Craziest Things*, I still believed that

Cast and crew of Who's the Boss? *celebrating the show's one hundredth episode*

being on-camera represented the next step in the evolution of my career, and I wanted greatly to make it happen.

When I told other members of the staff about what I was planning to do, they looked at me like I had totally lost it. Not because of the job I wanted to take or even because I was planning to leave the show, but because this would mean having to break the news to Danza. They told me he was going to be livid, as he believed in loyalty above all else. Everyone seemed to imply that they wouldn't trade places with me for all the money in the world (let alone a segment on a yet-to-even-air show hosted by some guy they'd never heard of).

I was given Danza's personal number; I hadn't had it before then. As was the case with most stars, not many did. Still, I could not simply call him at home out of the blue: I had to set up a time with his secretary when it would be okay to contact him. The formalities were piling up, which was making me even more nervous.

Finally, the time came. (Luckily, I had Geno in the room with me for moral support.) I nervously placed the call. Though we had always been on a first-name basis, the first thing Danza did when I simply said "hello" was shout into the phone: *"Perlow!"* like Mr. Spacely from *The Jetsons* or some other stereotypical mean cartoon boss.

"What's going on!" he demanded, in the same harsh tone. And this was before I had even got a word in beyond "hello"! I knew this tone: it was the one from the Show 7 catastrophe, which did not bode well for me.

At that moment I seriously contemplated forgetting the entire *House Party* thing and telling Danza I had just called to say "hi." (Like *that* would ever happen.) Finally, I told him as gently as I could about the offer in New York and how I was planning to leave his show to pursue it and (humbly) "I hope it's okay with you, Tony, okay?" (All the while I tried to emphasize that this could well be my "big break," praying that it would make a difference.)

Danza went even more ballistic. "No, it is *not* 'okay'!

What the *f—*, Perlow! Don't you know *nobody* leaves my show! Know what you are, Perlow? You're an f—ing *traitor*, that's what you are!" I think he said (yelled) some more stuff, but I had pretty much gone numb by that point. He slammed the phone down.

Needless to say, I was devastated. Even after all the warnings I'd gotten about Danza not taking the news well, I could not have been prepared for what I just got. I never imagined him having this extreme a reaction. What was going to happen to me as a result of this? I'd been in the business long enough to know that "You'll never eat lunch in this town again" wasn't just an idle threat. (And to be honest I was starting to get hungry.)

I figured I was already pretty much through as a TV writer, but now I wondered whether I would ever be able to do audience warmup again. No, forget that; would I ever work as a *tour guide* again? I had no idea how far Danza's powers extended, and now it looked like I was about to find out the hard way.

A few minutes later the phone rang again. This was before caller ID, so I just picked it up. I immediately heard Danza yelling "Perlow!" just as he had minutes earlier. I just thought, "Oh no! How much worse could this possibly get?"

Then, Danza let me off the hook, as his tone of voice did a complete 180-degree turn. "Bob," he started. (If nothing else, we were at least back to first names. Yay!) "Bob, I'm just kidding! I'm just busting your balls," he laughed. "I'd never hold you back. Best of luck with whatever you end up doing."

That was certainly a relief, to put it mildly. However, I did enjoy my time on *Who's the Boss?* And with this send off, I got my final reminder as to exactly who the boss was—and would always be.

The cast and crew of House Party with Steve Doocy

Chapter Sixteen

House Party with Steve Doocy

House Party was a variety/talk show hosted by Art Linkletter that began on radio in 1945. In 1950 it moved over to TV, where it would air for two decades, making it the longest-running daytime variety show ever. Then, in 1989, NBC Studio Productions, a new offshoot of NBC, launched a revival series that would also air in the morning, intended to compete with shows like *Live with Regis and Kathy Lee* but with perhaps a bit more emphasis on comedy.

I was a regular on this later version. I got to have my own segment and I was also the on-air cohost (well, sort of a cohost, which I'll explain) in the studio, in addition to doing the audience warmup. It's safe to say our version didn't do quite as well as Linkletter's original. *House Party with Steve Doocy*, as this incarnation was known, ran for just under a year of dismal ratings. Nonetheless, it was probably the most fulfilling and creative experience of my career up to that point.

In the fall of 1989, my agents had contacted me about a new show being put together by NBC Productions. They wanted me to provide some concepts for what could ultimately become my own on-air segment. I met with them and pitched about twenty-five or thirty different ideas. This included everything from having me comment on bad movies to simply filming me doing the audience warmup.

The one the producers liked the most and that we ultimately agreed upon (and which as it turned out also happened to be my favorite) was called "Let Bob Do It." The idea was that I would step in and perform various tasks for viewers who were unable or unwilling to do them themselves, with (hopefully) comedic results. I signed to do the show, and it was "game on."

Before being hired for the job, I had not been familiar with Steve Doocy, the man who would be hosting. This is okay because I don't think *anyone* was, unless they lived in the Washington, DC, area, where he had been a field news correspondent for the local NBC affiliate. I'm still not sure how this made him qualified to host a national comedy-laden morning talk show. (As it turned out, it *didn't*.)

A potentially better omen was the fact that we would be taping the show in Studio 8H at 30 Rockefeller Center. If that location sounds familiar, it's because it's where *Saturday Night Live* has originated from since Chevy Chase took his first pratfall in 1975. *House Party* was done live-to-tape, which means that it was shot straight through, with minimal—or no—retakes, as though the show were airing live. So we would have the studio from Sunday to Wednesday (doing five days' worth of shows), and then *SNL* (who were in the middle of the classic Dana Carvey/Phil Hartman/Mike Myers period) would take over for the rest of the week.

What seemed most promising about *House Party*—or so I thought—was that it was going to be produced by Barry Sand, who had been David Letterman's producer for fifteen years. But it turns out there were things about Sand that no one who signed on for *House Party* (including me) had been told, beginning with the fact that during the last part of his Letterman tenure Sand had come to be considered, to put it cordially, irrational. And some have used stronger adjectives than that.

In and of itself, that may depend on whom you ask. However, during his last two years with Letterman, Sand had been barred from any and all show staff meetings and kept out of all significant decision making; this part was undisputed fact.

I tried to focus purely on the show, since this was going to be by far the most time I had ever spent in front of the camera. But old habits die hard: I was still doing the audience warmup for *House Party*. While not officially the cohost, I did end up being Doocy's on-camera sidekick, as we would occasionally do a back-and-forth with him onstage and me standing out among the people in the bleachers. The way it was shot was kind of similar to the David Letterman/Paul Shaffer dynamic. So I suppose I was sort of Shaffer Light, minus the music.

I did my "Let Bob Do It" segments, which I'll discuss in detail in the next chapter. However, the show also allowed me to do other, self-contained segments on occasion. For example, during that period it was reported that billionaire and future presidential candidate Donald Trump was having "financial troubles" as a result of the real estate bust of '89-'90 (which for him meant he could still buy the world but might have to pay in installments).

So with the assistance of a volunteer from the audience, I took the camera crew out to the street, set up a Salvation Army-type donation bucket, and rang a bell, calling out, "Help the Donald!" Quite a few passers-by actually stopped to offer contributions!

That money went—no, not to Trump (Donald, if you're reading this, please don't send lawyers after us!)—but to a legitimate charity. I don't remember which one exactly. But in hindsight maybe we should've just kept it; *House Party* was getting clobbered in the ratings.

In spite of this, we did get a few name guests booked on the show. One time Billy Dee Williams was on and was sitting backstage in the green room, which most people know is where guests on a talk show hang out while they're waiting to do their on-air segment. Ours was never even actually green.

One of the producers walked in and changed the monitor in the room for him to see a live feed of our show in progress. Williams apparently got upset over this, since he had been watching one of his favorite daytime shows.

Musical guests we found to be a mixed bag. Tony Bennett did the show but asked that he not have to sing. By sharp contrast, Mel Tormé (my old buddy from his countless *Night Court* appearances) insisted on three segments, all of which would include a song. Both of them would get what they wanted—being a legend does give one a certain amount of leeway.

On the subject of music, actor Werner Klemperer was working as a conductor (his father was the great German conductor Otto Klemperer) and had an upcoming concert that he wanted to plug, which was the only reason he agreed to do our show. Despite the musical career that represented his true passion, Klemperer was best known—okay, let's face it, *only* known—for his role as Colonel Wilhelm Klink on the Sixties sitcom *Hogan's Heroes.*

Klemperer agreed to do *House Party* only on the further condition that no reference—none whatsoever—be made to *Hogan's Heroes.* Under the circumstances this clearly seemed like a tall order. Still, our producers had supposedly said they *would* comply with this stipulation weeks earlier, when the appearance was first booked.

Doocy apparently either missed the memo or chose to ignore it. You would think he would at least wait until Klemperer seemed at ease with the interview before maybe slipping *Hogan's* into the conversation in some tactful manner. *Nope.* No sooner had Klemperer sat down than Doocy asked him, "So what was Bob Crane like?" referring to the star of the show who had been murdered under tawdry circumstances in 1978. Klemperer kept his composure during the interview but predictably left the studio in a huff, uttering "that bastard!" in his German accent and slamming every door behind him.

Apparently, people who starred on hit TV shows in the Sixties don't like being reminded of it. When Peter Graves, star of the original *Mission: Impossible* (no, that wasn't Tom Cruise) did the show, he turned up at the studio drunk.

He headed right for one of our producers, whom Graves, at six-foot-four, absolutely towered over. "No matter what," Graves told him, "no *Mission: Impossible* jokes! No parody!

No *ridicule!*" We honored the request, figuring it was better than having Graves self-destruct in five seconds (or try to kill Steve Forrest, the producer responsible for booking guests).

There were a number of talented regulars and semi-regulars on the show as well. Rosie O'Donnell—who was still known mostly as a stand-up comic—would come on about once a month to read (and make jokes about) absurd tabloid headlines. Not celebrity gossip, but the *really* fun ones from *The Weekly World News*, which were usually about things like aliens, werewolves, and bigfoots . . . wait, or is that "bigfeet"?

There was also Nely Galán, a hottie who would do a regular "What's New" (in terms of fashion, etc.) segment. Galán's on-camera persona was that of a "lovable bimbo," being sort of Charo-esque. (How's that for an addition to the list of eponymous adjectives? *Shakespearean. Dickensian. Charo-esque.*) However, Galán was apparently smarter than she wanted any of us to realize, since she would eventually end up as president of entertainment at Telemundo, the most successful Spanish-language TV network in the United States.

Another regular was Paul Prudhomme, the famous chef who strongly resembled actor Dom DeLuise (more on the real DeLuise in a future chapter). Generally considered to be one of the greatest chefs in the world, Prudhomme was originally booked to do—logically enough—cooking segments.

However, Barry Sand saw Prudhomme as sort of a "freak" (his word exactly) based on his physical appearance. Though seriously, would anyone trust a chef who was too thin? Prudhomme did openly acknowledge at the time that he was dieting, so Sand insisted that we weigh him on the air every week. Even though this may be where the idea for *Celebrity Fit Club* came from, it was an example of just how much Sand, at the time, was losing it just as he had on the Letterman show.

During this period, Sand would mostly lock himself in his office with his "producer." This would be Gayle Silverman, the woman he had left his wife for. When Sand first met her,

Silverman had been his dental hygienist, and apparently he decided she was capable of eliminating more than tartar; he would send her to do most of the firing of employees when deemed necessary.

Silverman would soon come to be known as "the most powerful dental hygienist in show business." But apparently even this kind of (unprecedented) power had potential for abuse. She apparently fired *House Party* director Bob Levy by leaving him a note (the exact content has never been disclosed, though most accounts suggest it included the words "worthless piece of s—" and/or "s—ty director"). Either way, it must have been a dilly. Levy sued the production company and ended up winning a substantial settlement.

With Silverman doing the firing (ostensibly not very well), it stood to reason that she would also be doing the hiring. Apparently this included a psychic named Yolanda—no, not to appear on-camera, just to advise the two of them on how to run the show. They clearly should've hired a better one, as the ratings for *House Party* continued to slip. Finally, after about a year on the air, the show ended unceremoniously.

In yet another bizarre twist that could only happen in the world of television, Steve Doocy would end up as an ultra-right wing commentator as host of *Fox and Friends* on the Fox News Channel (keep in mind, this is someone who had once been intended to be direct competition for Kathy Lee Gifford).

Today, *House Party* is barely remembered. Back in LA, I would resume my career as a warmup comic (as you'll be reading about in subsequent chapters). But miserable ratings can't tell me I didn't have the time of my life doing that show. In the next chapter I'll be explaining some of the reasons why—plus how, over a decade after *House Party* ended, my "Let Bob Do It" concept got a second chance . . . sort of.

Chapter Seventeen

Let Bob Do It

What? You never heard of it? Neither have most people. Let me explain.

On *House Party with Steve Doocy*, I may have been the comic relief quasi de-facto cohost, if only by process of elimination (plus we couldn't get anyone else who wanted to do it). However, I was nobody's second banana when it came to the show's weekly "Let Bob Do It" segments . . . mainly because *I'm* Bob.

Just to reiterate briefly: the idea of the segment was that I, Bob, would step in to do tasks or activities that people would rather not do themselves. We tried our best to diversify the themes of the outings: One week I had to give a toast at the wedding of a couple I had never met before. I became a Girl Scout leader for a day (where I ended up getting the troop lost in the woods). I made pizza, tossing it in the air, sometimes catching it, sometimes not (*two-second rule!*). And I even spent a day as the operator of a grain elevator.

One of my favorite segments we ever did (and unquestionably among the best) involved me becoming the mayor of the town of Krum, Texas (population less than 1,500) for one day. I was to do the job while the real elected mayor was gone for the afternoon. (He was actually gone most afternoons; he had a full-time position at the Coca-Cola bottling plant in nearby Dallas.)

I put on a cowboy hat, which made me look very mayoral (for Texas, at least) and taller (which is also good for Texas, where *babies* start at six feet). The local sheriff gave me a tour, of which one of the highlights was the local public library. A public library that was, in fact, a *trailer*.

The sheriff introduced me as "the new mayor" to the librarian—who, on the off chance I actually *had* any power that day, told me that she had been asking city hall to give her a back door for the "library" for quite some time. When I pointed out the obvious (It's a trailer!) she said that didn't make any difference: not having a back door still created a fire hazard for the twenty to thirty children who would visit daily and in an emergency would have only one way out.

At that point, I started to go a little mad with power. Think Napoleon. I called NBC and got them to release enough money (about eight hundred dollars) to have local carpenters and technicians come over right away and put the much-needed back door on the trailer/library.

I asked the sheriff if he knew a carpenter who might be capable of installing a door on the "library." In something right out of *The Andy Griffith Show*, he called to someone who happened to be right across the street at that moment and asked him, "Billy! Think you can do a door for the library?"

Then, we got a beekeeper involved. Hold on, I'll explain: Billy (!) had to wait to install the door until an active beehive could be removed from the back of the "library." Whether the door couldn't be installed up until then because of the beehive or the beehive was there because no one had gotten around to putting in the door, I'm still not sure. But what I do know is that this required the skills of a beekeeper. Fortunately, there was one of those around, too—Billy's cousin Joe, who was getting a haircut next door (this *was* a small town).

Wait . . . there's more. It gets worse. Once the door was installed, I thought, "What's the most mayor-y thing I could do to celebrate this victory?" And it hit me: have a parade, of course! I called the high school and had them send over the marching band and cheerleaders, and six teenagers who were wearing dusters and riding horses.

I got tractors to be in it and even got the town's former librarian—who was now about ninety years old—to ride in the back of a pickup truck as sort of the grand marshal. And just like that, I had a parade down Main Street (or whatever the actual name of the street was; I'm still guessing "Main"). All this in an eight-hour period. I should've legitimately been the mayor.

I was so much basking in the glory that it's a good thing I wasn't there longer or I just might have had a statue erected of myself (hmm . . . wonder if it's too late). But my bubble was about to burst at around six p.m. This was when the real mayor got back from Dallas, because like most people, his work day had ended at five p.m.

He was okay with the parade and even the ribbon cutting ceremony (yes, there was one of those too), but not so much with the reason (other than my ego) for them. He told me that the back door for the library had been a hot issue for quite some time (again, this was a very small town), and by my addressing it in the swift, decisive manner that I did, I made him look bad.

This had not been my intention. After all, this man was not just a Coca-Cola bottler and had been truly dedicated to something that I was only really pretending to do in front of the cameras for one day. I was able to save his reputation by allowing everyone to believe that the door had been his idea all along. Seemingly, it worked. To show his gratitude, he issued a plaque to me which still adorns my wall in Rhode Island.

Also, after the segment aired, the producers got a very nice letter from the librarian thanking us for bringing the show to their little town, saying that everyone watched it when it aired and tried to spot their relatives. There was also a thank-you note with signatures from about 150 Klum citizens. It was very gratifying.

After getting back from Texas, I knew it might be tough to top that one, although I almost certainly would have if I had responded to a request that had come from a prison inmate who had been incarcerated in upstate New York. He was on death row, and he wanted me to take his place there. Interestingly, he didn't specify that he wanted me to do it on the day the execution was scheduled. But needless to say, we had to take a pass (but what a great show business exit it would have been).

I didn't get very many requests to do anything particularly physical, let alone dangerous, because that wasn't really the point of the segment. I'm an improv comic, not a stuntman. This was before *Jackass* or any of those extreme stunt reality shows came in and tried to make personal injury the object of ridicule.

However, I did get a request from someone who said that he had lost a bet and wanted me to take his place (even though I'm pretty sure that constitutes "welching"). What he wanted me to do (instead of him) was join the Polar Bear Club for a day. If you're not familiar with them, it's the most famous organization in the United States dedicated to ice swimming.

Wait—what? *Ice swimming?*

Ice swimming—unfortunately—is pretty much what it sounds like. Well, not so much the "swimming" part. It often involves simply getting into the water, albeit in the middle of winter, when the water is in fact icy cold, wearing nothing but regular bathing suits.

The Polar Bears were based out of Coney Island and included both men and women (all adults). Quite a few were European immigrants, which makes sense because ice swimming is more popular in Europe (although then again, so is pickled herring, thus the whole there's-no-accounting-for-taste thing).

Although there are some organizations that make the ice swimming an annual event, the Polar Bears pull out all the stops, swimming every Sunday during the winter. They don't go swimming during the summer, because of course that would be ridiculous.

On New Year's Day 1990, I went to Coney Island Beach, where I would be participating. I got ready to jump into the icy cold water. I was a bit reluctant to say the least, and I demanded of NBC and anyone who would listen that there be a doctor and an ambulance standing by. This is despite the fact that I was with several dozen people who were all about to do the exact same thing. So imagine how I felt when most of them got off a city bus, disrobed, and ran right into the water like a bunch of lemmings with me feeling like the biggest wuss in the world, still on the shore.

But reluctantly (and eventually) I followed, and while the water was unquestionably freezing, once I got used to it, it wasn't quite as bad as I'd imagined. It was worse. Even so, in terms of my health concerns, my problem ended up being not hypothermia but hypochondria: all I ended up getting was the sniffles (which hardly requires an ambulance). And the look of distain from ten large Russian men who, when they saw I had an ambulance standing by in case I caught cold, just sadly shook their heads at this, murmuring, "Soft American . . ."

During the show's end credits, there would be a call for suggestions for the "Let Bob Do It" segment, along with the address of where viewers could send the letters (no e-mail quite yet). Most of the suggestions we got were not quite as imaginative as we'd hoped for. A lot of people just asked me to do something mundane, like walk their dog or clear the leaves out of their rain gutters. One of the most confusing trends was that right after any segment aired, for the next three weeks we would get requests to do something very similar or even identical. So either they were unimaginative or I did a very good job (I'm guessing the former).

Although it may have been a bit of a deviation from the segment's underlying concept, one of the most satisfying ones we did involved fulfilling the dream of an eighty-six-year-old woman who, because of her age and health, had trouble getting around. We took her on a trip to Atlantic City, where we made sure she got the full VIP treatment. We told everyone we met on the shoot that the woman had won the lottery. I suppose in a sense she did.

Me, not so much. As described in the last chapter, *House Party* crashed and burned after less than a year (ratings were so low in some markets the producers had to call the local affiliates to make sure the show was actually airing), taking my segment with it. I figured that was the end of "Let Bob Do It."

Then around January 2002, I got a call from Jason Alexander. Yes, the same Jason Alexander who will be forever known the world over as George Costanza from *Seinfeld*. We had been friends since we'd met years earlier, when he had been a cast member and I was doing warmup for *E/R*. (No, not *that ER*. This one was a sitcom, although George Clooney was on both—it's confusing, I realize.)

With *Seinfeld* recently ending its historic run, Alexander had just formed a production company and was looking for projects. He remembered the "Let Bob Do It" segments on *House Party* (he had attended several tapings) and wanted to know if I might be interested in turning it into its own show.

Of course, before we could move forward, he needed to know if I had the rights to the "Let Bob Do It" title and concept. Truthfully, it had been so long that I wasn't even sure myself at that point. And I wished that someone else had *really* been offering a "Let Bob Do It"-type service (Let Kevin Do It? Let Raheem Do It?) that I could take advantage of to help me find out, because doing so turned into a colossal headache.

Securing the full rights to "Let Bob Do It" wasn't so much complicated as time-consuming, as well as extremely frustrating. NBC dragged their feet, even though they knew that I knew perfectly well that they had no further use for "Let Bob Do It" and no reason to keep it from me (say nothing of the fact that I was collaborating with the costar of one of their all-time biggest hits). Nonetheless, they didn't want it to look like they were "giving" me anything, so all in all the rights took about six months to clear.

So finally in possession of the rights, we went ahead with shopping *Let Bob Do It* as a self-contained half-hour show. It was, I believe, one of the first hybrid reality/scripted shows. But TV networks aren't interested in pioneers, mostly only in shows that can be explained in a few words, and ours was not one of them.

Bob with Jason Alexander

Bob with George Clooney

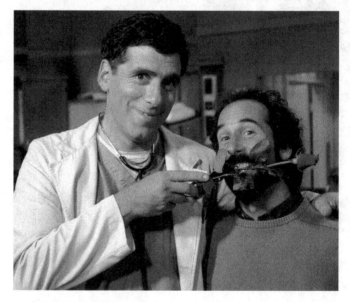

Bob with Elliot Gould on the set of the sitcom E/R

Nonetheless, we forged ahead, using Alexander's name and *Seinfeld* clout as the front. The networks all passed on the project (including, ironically, NBC) but ultimately we got an offer from Viacom-owned cable network Nickelodeon. They expressed interest in possibly airing the show as part of their evening and overnight block Nick at Nite.

Since the mid-Eighties, Nick at Nite had been airing almost entirely reruns—mostly sitcoms, everything from *Green Acres* to *Mary Tyler Moore*. The twist was that rather than treating these shows like cheap airtime filler, they presented all of them—even generally ridiculed shows like *Car 54, Where Are You?*—as cherished classics. However, they had produced very, very few original shows, and none of those had been successful.

Still, they agreed to underwrite the cost of our show, in those days usually just north of a million dollars, to go shoot the pilot for *Let Bob Do It*.

The next order of business was casting the part of Bob. Yes, I know, it sounds weird, since Bob is not only my name but I was the "Bob" in the original *House Party* segments. I created him, for crying out loud. But Alexander and I agreed that someone else should be on camera this time. Particularly since we were doing this show for an arm of Nickelodeon, which was a network aimed at children, "Bob" should be someone a bit younger (that's Hollywood for you—I had been aged out of the role of myself).

We cast a young improv comic named Larry Dorf as "Bob." Dorf had done a few TV appearances and would go on to small roles in comedy films like *Evan Almighty* and *Tammy*. But nobody was about to keep me completely off camera, either: Alexander and I played the show's producers in the wrap-around segments.

Of course, since nothing had aired yet, we couldn't put out a public call for suggestions the way we had on *House Party*. So instead we went with the more primitive methods of getting the word out, putting up fliers on telephone poles and taking out classified ads in the paper in the Los Angeles area.

Bob with "new Bob" Larry Dorf

Bob with Larry Dorf (left) and Jason Alexander (right)

The fliers and ads read something along the lines of "Got something you'd rather not do? Why not let Bob do it?" We didn't indicate that it was for a TV show. The response we got was a bit underwhelming, but we had at least enough material to do the pilot.

We did two segments on the show of Larry, a.k.a "Bob," stepping in for someone else. The first involved him at a wedding filling in for the groom (the groom knew he was going to be late but the guests didn't). The other one provided a nice—if potentially dangerous—contrast: here, "Bob" went skydiving.

But apparently even this wasn't enough to impress Nickelodeon (or at least not the test audiences they used who probably decided our final fate), since despite the seven-figure investment they decided to pass on the show. As is usually the case, we never got any specific reasons, just the polite show business brush-offs (i.e., "We love, love, love it! It's just not what we're looking for right now").

The half-hour pilot never aired, and that was essentially the end of "Let Bob Do It." If there's a silver lining, it's that the failure of the half-hour version, featuring another "Bob," means that the *House Party* segments, which I appeared on, remain the true manifestation of this concept. Those segments are still among the favorite moments of my entire career. Even though the whole idea was for me to trade places with other people, for the year I did those segments I would never have traded places with anyone else.

Bob with Bonnie Raitt

Chapter Eighteen

The Rock and Roll Hall of Fame Induction Ceremony

My sitcom writing partner, Geno, had played the drums in a few small-time rock bands before we worked together. I, on the other hand, never really had much in the way of musical aspirations. As a kid growing up in Rhode Island, I took up the trumpet briefly but quit after a short time because I didn't have the discipline to learn how to read music. (And anyway . . . seriously, the trumpet?)

A few years later, I learned the bass drum—not even the full drum kit, just the bass drum. This time, I actually stuck with the instrument long enough to develop a repertoire that was composed of one song, "The Merry Widow Waltz."

Obviously, none of this very, very limited musical experience exactly screams "Rock and Roll." Still, the very next time I picked up a musical instrument, I would be playing alongside Bruce Springsteen, Simon and Garfunkel, The Who, Diana Ross, U2, Bonnie Raitt, James Taylor, and other huge names. And all at the same time.

It was the induction ceremony for the Rock and Roll Hall of Fame in 1990, which took place in New York City at the Waldorf Astoria on January 17. I was living in New York at the time doing *House Party*. What I did at the Hall of Fame ceremony could well have been a "Let Bob Do It" stunt—and it was even televised. The only difference is that no one had requested that I do what I did, and in fact they would've been happier if I hadn't.

One of the *House Party* producers, Amy, happened to have an extra ticket to the event and asked me if I wanted to join her. I wasn't doing anything else that night and of course it seemed pretty exciting, so I agreed to go.

We got there and sat through all the inductions and the speeches. The acts who made the Hall of Fame that year included not only The Who and Simon and Garfunkel but also The Kinks, The Four Tops, The Platters, The Four Seasons, and (posthumously) Bobby Darin. Springsteen, Diana Ross, James Taylor, Boz Scaggs, and the members of U2 were among those on hand to do the inductions. Providing backup for all the night's music was the house band from *Late Night with David Letterman*, led by Paul Shaffer.

As a card-carrying member of the Baby Boomer generation, it was pretty thrilling seeing many of the musicians I had grown up with there, and being acknowledged for all the amazing and timeless work that they had done. Still, the evening had its ups and downs: Phil Spector got up to give a speech that was meant to induct The Platters, but he began going off on so many tangents that he was finally asked to leave the stage. In hindsight this may have spoken to Spector's deteriorating mental state (in 2009 he would end up in prison after being convicted of murdering a woman).

One thing I did not see while I was there, however, was much in the way of security. This event had not been open to the general public; one needed to be fairly closely connected to the music business in order to gain admittance. So they probably figured that in spite of all the big names there that night, anyone who was in attendance would be self-disciplined enough to behave themselves.

Little did they know.

Once the main part of the program was done, there was an intermission of sorts as they began preparations for the evening's finale, which was something they had been doing since these annual ceremonies had started four years earlier: the all-star jam, in which the inductees present, as well as the evening's presenters and others, would all get up on stage and perform together, usually doing a medley of well-known songs by the inductees.

Amy decided to seize this lull in the evening's proceedings as an opportunity to go get another drink; she excused herself, got up, and walked towards the bar on the other side of the room. What I ended up doing with this downtime would prove to be just a bit more foolhardy.

For a while by that point, I had been studying the stage: it was just a few feet off the ground, with a small staircase leading up from the floor. There was a grand piano, and I found myself focusing more and more on a tambourine that was lying on top of it.

After all those years of working on *Laverne & Shirley*, the mantra of the show's theme song, "making our dreams come true," was now racing through my consciousness. I could make at least one of my dreams come true, and that tambourine was the ticket. Taking all of these factors into consideration, I made my decision; I would get up there on stage and be part of the all-star jam along with all these legendary music figures!

It probably helped—or *didn't* help, depending on how you look at things—that a couple of years earlier I had done *People Do the Craziest Things*. In one episode, they had me in a diner where I would just brazenly walk up to patrons and start eating their food. At the time, for whatever reason, none of these people told me to stop, or even appeared to take any sort of issue with what was going on. Doing things like this had perhaps made me a bit over-confident in my ability to infiltrate situations where I didn't belong.

So as casually as I could, I got up and made my way onto the stage, trying my best to be inconspicuous. In preparation for what was being planned, a number of other people were also going up to the stage (people who were actually supposed to be there), so I managed to blend in with the "crowd."

Once on stage, I immediately—and in my best Indiana Jones move—grabbed the tambourine and held onto it. The instrument became the final part of my "disguise." I was dressed like just about everyone else there, and even my hair at the time was a reasonable length by Rock and Roll standards circa 1990. So far, so good.

A few minutes later, the playing began. Not a moment too

soon, either, since it was less likely anyone would be willing to disrupt the music in order to have me removed from the situation.

I would actually manage to stay up on that stage for the whole jam, during which the medley would include short versions of songs such as "Mack the Knife," "You Really Got Me," "Will You Love Me Tomorrow," and "Pinball Wizard." All the while, I continued to hit—er, *play*—the tambourine, which I was able to strike on the beat for pretty much the entire duration. I guess the time I spent on that bass drum in junior high went further than I thought.

This was fortunate, because I needed to reserve half my attention to looking out for one certain individual: Bill Graham, the organizer of the event. Anyone of my generation knew all about Graham, the legendary concert promoter who would elevate live Rock and Roll to previously unheard-of scales.

However, that wasn't the part that concerned me: Graham was also widely reputed for having a dangerously short temper, potentially exacerbated by anyone who had the nerve to in any way disrupt something he was involved with (me jumping on the stage very much uninvited would probably qualify). Graham most likely would not have thought twice about having me thrown out on the sidewalk (or worse).

So during the songs, whenever I caught Graham in my line of sight, I would take one or two steps back so as to better blend into the crowd. But every time I thought the coast was clear, I was able to get back to the front, which I later found out even Diana Ross (someone else whom conventional wisdom says it's best not to anger) had not been able to do.

Once the music was finished, I placed the tambourine back on the piano where I found it (hey, give me that much credit). Then I turned around, and I was suddenly face-to-face with exactly the person I had been hoping to avoid: Bill Graham. His expression suggested he was about as happy to see me up there as I had figured he'd be.

"*Who the f— are you!*" he demanded to know.

I simply replied (truthfully, in fact): "I'm the guy who's leaving the stage." And that's exactly what I did. Quickly.

I then found Amy so she and I could make an abrupt exit together. She told me that when she got back from the bar with her drink she wondered where I had gone to, and then she was amazed to look at the video monitors and spot me playing the tambourine. All she said to me was, "I can't believe they let Bob do that!"

She wasn't the only one, as it turns out. I assumed I'd never hear another word about my little escapade; however, the very next night I happened to be watching *Late Night with David Letterman*. Since Paul Shaffer and the rest of the show's band had been there, it was a safe bet that the ceremony might be mentioned during the episode.

One of the night's guests was the author Fran Lebowitz. During her interview, it came up that she too had attended the

Bob (fourth from left) and his "band": Bruce Springsteen, Pete Townshend, Michael Bolton, Diana Ross, Phil Spector, Art Garfunkel, Paul Shaffer, Rickie Lee Jones, Phoebe Snow, Boz Scaggs, Carole King, and more

event. I hadn't remembered seeing her there. But apparently she very much saw, and remembered, me.

LETTERMAN: Any isolated events you can comment on from last night?

LEBOWITZ: I don't know if Paul noticed this but there was an imposter on the stage. [Turns to Shaffer] Did you see that guy?

SHAFFER: Yes. Yes.

LEBOWITZ: I was the first to notice him.

SHAFFER: A guy who had no business being there.

LEBOWITZ: Had no business being *anywhere*. [Audience laughs] I mean, there were a thousand rock stars on the stage, and this one guy who stood out because he looked more like, kind of, an aspiring accountant.

LETTERMAN: Uh-huh . . .

LEBOWITZ: He had a tambourine, and he was one of those people who was, like, shaking his tambourine in a very . . . *unseemly* manner, pointing to other people telling them what to do. And I kept saying: "Who's that guy? Get that guy off the stage." And he would slither over. First he was next to Boz Scaggs, then Diana Ross, then he slithered over next to Bruce Springsteen—that's where they nabbed him.

LETTERMAN: Oh, really. So this guy was just a crasher then, huh, Paul?

SHAFFER: Just a crasher, yeah.

LETTERMAN: Is this the first year this has ever happened?

SHAFFER: First time I've ever noticed it, yeah.

LETTERMAN: Maybe one day he'll be inducted into the Hall of Fame, when they get down to the end of the list.

Despite congratulating herself on "busting" me, Lebowitz didn't get the whole story right. First of all, if I "pointed" to anyone, it certainly wasn't in an effort to try and tell them what they should be doing. I was brave, not (necessarily) crazy. Also, as I recounted earlier, nobody actually "nabbed" me (close call though it was).

In saying that I looked like an "aspiring accountant," well, I do have a master's degree in business, so maybe Lebowitz was at least in the ballpark. The "slithering" part of the story that she described was, admittedly, right on point.

Still, just who was this woman to claim that I had "no business being anywhere"? Although I was taking a break from it to do *House Party*, I was still probably most successful warmup man in Hollywood, thank you very much, and was soon to begin my thirteen years with *The Tonight Show*.

Given all this, one might expect that Paul Shaffer, at least, would know who I was. He did have pretty much equal footing in music and comedy, having been a member of the house band (and occasional performer) on the original *Saturday Night Live* before joining Letterman in 1982.

Yet I had never worked (at least not officially) on any show or project that Shaffer was involved with. To this day, I've never even met him. Part of this was because with the exception of this short period, almost my entire career had been spent in Los Angeles. I had very little direct connection to Letterman, *SNL*, or other comedy originating out of the East Coast (this was also before the Internet, which made the gap even wider).

Further, more concise evidence of my little stunt surfaced about two weeks later, when the March 8 issue of *Rolling Stone* came out. There appeared a group photo taken during the jam, including a clear image of me in all my glory. Looking at the picture, Shaffer seems to be pointing at me, and could possibly be saying, "Who's that?" (Not to mention Pete Townshend from The Who, standing above me, almost appearing to be eyeing me suspiciously.)

After that, the incident was, in fact, largely forgotten. However, when I began doing my one-man show in 2011, through contacts I was able to obtain video from the ceremony of me playing onstage. People have asked me if the film is real or if it's all just part of a comedy bit that I concocted utilizing *Forrest Gump*-type computer technology to incorporate myself into the footage (based on the rest of my show, I can't imagine how anyone figures I was working with that kind of budget).

Yet proof of sorts exists in another form: as of the following year's ceremony, there was no more all-star jam. I've made an educated guess that I am the reason that this practice was discontinued. No more closing the Rock and Roll Hall of Fame inductions with a spontaneous musical mash-up between all the musicians who are there.

The Rock and Roll Hall of Fame does include a category for the people who aren't actually musicians—Sam Phillips, Alan Freed, Berry Gordy, Dick Clark—but who have still, through some action, made a lasting impact on Rock and Roll. If someone ever decides that what I did that night (i.e. killing the all-star jam forever) qualifies, then maybe Letterman's prediction of me being inducted into the Hall will come to pass. Not likely, but the whole experience was pretty thrilling.

Chapter Nineteen

Candid Camera

Candid Camera wasn't just a TV show or even a TV franchise. It was an American institution. Alan Funt originally started the show on radio before bringing it to TV during the medium's stone age in 1948, utilizing the simple idea of catching the reaction of ordinary people in humorous situations who didn't know they were being filmed.

The show soon became an inescapable part of popular culture. The slogan "Smile, you're on *Candid Camera*," used to inform the people that they were being filmed, became (and would remain) a national catchphrase. It would also become commonplace for people in everyday life to ask out loud, "Am I on *Candid Camera*?" when faced with a situation seemingly too absurd to be true.

Funt would produce and host numerous versions of *Candid Camera* up through the Seventies. As no copyright law protected the basic hidden-camera idea (hide a camera and turn it on . . . that can hardly be patented), dozens of knock-off versions would pop up in the English-speaking world alone. I had even appeared on one such variation, *People Do the Craziest Things*, in 1984 (see chapter eleven).

Several years later, the producers of *Craziest Things* decided to give the *Candid Camera* format another whirl, this time offering it legitimacy by buying the rights to the name (and hopefully not repeating the mistake of having it air opposite first-run episodes of *The Cosby Show*).

For me, the beginning of the Nineties would be a somewhat difficult period career-wise. By leaving my story editor job on *Who's the Boss?* and moving to New York City to do *House*

Party, I had essentially put all my chips on one number. But I wasn't worried. After that show failed, I returned to Los Angeles, thinking that I would immediately be able to go back to doing audience warmup and just pick up again where I left off.

Not so fast, Bob. Welcome to show biz, *yet again*. It turned out to be a little more complicated than that. No, scratch that: it was actually very simple. As with all careers, there have to be positions available, and at this time I found there were just no audience warmup jobs open, not even for someone with my experience and a solid reputation. I had always showed up on time, made 'em laugh and never left early . . . but none of this was going to get blood out of a stone.

Thus I was relieved and thankful to get the call from the producers whom I had worked with on *Craziest Things* about this new show. Not only would it would be *Candid Camera*, a brand name that all TV viewers knew already, but this incarnation would be airing five nights a week. I would be doing the same thing I had done on their other show: being on camera and setting the pranks up so that we would be able to catch and film the people's responses.

The potentially bad news was that this would be the first version of *Candid Camera* where Alan Funt would have no direct involvement. The show would be hosted by Dom DeLuise, the rotund and exceptionably likable actor who'd been a favorite in feature films, where he was mainly known for his on-screen pairings with Burt Reynolds and appearances in Mel Brooks comedies.

The show would not begin airing until 1991, but we spent the better part of a year before that filming the segments all over the country. The reason we front-loaded the material this way was so that we could truly take people by surprise, which we thought might be more difficult if it were to become known that *Candid Camera* was at large once again.

Although we went out with a small group of players, I quickly become the most-used on-camera performer. This was probably because my combined experience as a tour guide and a warmup comic meant that I was capable of interacting comfortably, humorously, and most importantly on the fly with just about any random, total stranger (that and the fact that they soon rediscovered, as I had exhibited on *Craziest Things*, that I had no shame and would be willing to do nearly anything while it was being filmed). Yes, I was ready to humiliate myself for my craft.

I would end up being on the road for the better part of a year, but it was hardly a gypsy's existence (or what I had to go through way back when as a bus tour guide). We were usually put up in first-class hotels and fed the best meals (this was due largely to the strength of the actors' union).

We would spent a lot of time in smaller cities like Tucson and St. Louis and were routinely treated like royalty: when a TV show comes to pretty much anywhere in Middle America, even a small city, it's as though the circus has come to town (though our "circus" was pretty much only clowns). The perks alone made it one of the best jobs I ever had.

Bob with host Dom DeLuise

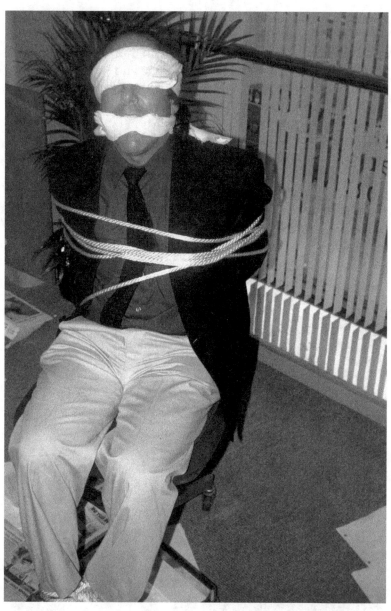

Ready for a segment involving a staged robbery—too bad the police didn't get the "staged" part

After rushing in with guns drawn, these officers realize they're on Candid Camera

A nerd getting ready to take a driving test

Two actors in an Arizona "shower phone booth"

An angry peace guru

Playing a sleazy salesman—easy

Who would help this "lady" in distress?

Shooting the segments, however, could be a bit difficult, because the ratio of bits that worked to ones that didn't was roughly ten to one (although they were almost all fun). Among the many that I did, one of the most memorable involved me being in a full-body cast. We would call a taxi, and on arrival I told the driver that it was urgent that I get where I needed to go. However, the way my arms and legs were positioned, it was impossible to get me through the car doors.

Many of the drivers would outright refuse service until I told them I was the brother of the local district attorney and it would be illegal and racist (I was white at the time) to refuse me service (and they bought that). One driver tried to "solve" this by putting me in the trunk, while another attempted to strap me to the roof using bungee cords!

Being put in the full-body cast took the crew five hours, and yet that didn't end up being the day's low point. It was very hot, as we were shooting outdoors in San Francisco in July, and since I was unable to move my arms, I asked a production assistant—let's call him "Jerry" ('cause that was his name)—if he would be willing to put his hat on me for a while as I was baking in the sun.

Well, Jerry refused the request, saying he was afraid the he "might not get it back." Apparently I signed a contract and committed to go out on the road with this show for a year all for the purpose of stealing this guy's hat, which was probably worth around seven bucks (though honestly it was so hot that day I might have given him a hundred for it).

When the show went to the bigger cities, such as LA or Chicago, we would often recruit local performers to help set up some of the segments. One person we "discovered" in New York City would help me on camera with a bit where I played a push-cart vender, and he had to squirt ketchup or mustard on the hot dogs . . . from a third-story window. My shill for this segment was a young, untapped talent named Kevin James, the future star of *The King of Queens* and feature films such as *Paul Blart: Mall Cop*.

Any of the marks, or "average people" who ended up on

Bob and Kevin James as "cops" during a segment

camera, had to sign a release form for us to be legally allowed to use the footage on the air. Our goal was always to get them to sign without having to offer any additional compensation (that's just the way the entertainment business operates, sad to say).

We would bring them into our mobile control room, which was located in a van parked discreetly hidden somewhere on the streets. Depending on whether our participant was a man or a woman, they would be greeted by our best-looking male or female staff member. We would then sit them down in front of the monitor and let them watch the footage of themselves.

That's when the snow would start falling, as that great-looking opposite-sex staff member would really lay it on thick in an attempt to get them to sign the release with no further obligation to us. Sounding nothing less than 100 percent sincere, they would tell them things like "Wow, you look amazing!" "You look like a movie star!" "I'll be surprised if you don't get a contract out of this!" etc. while they were both looking at the monitors.

So we were telling everyone just how flawless they looked in what was supposed to be this warts-and-all depiction of people being caught off-guard. Still, it *worked*, because in most cases that alone was enough to persuade them to happily sign the release. Keep in mind, this was well before everybody carried a portable device that they could use to film themselves and instantly post it to a forum where everyone on the planet could see it. Back then, people simply loved the idea of getting to be on TV (unless they were being arrested on *Cops*).

If all the flattery somehow missed the mark, we would go right to—I'm sorry to say—*begging*. After that, we would offer them a "prize" . . . a *Candid Camera* souvenir coin that we had minted and told them was a "limited edition." We neglected to mention how "limited"—we actually produced a "limited" slew of those coins. Look for mine on eBay. If the coin somehow didn't dazzle them, then we would go to plan C, as in "c-note": we would offer them up to a hundred dollars (we'd start with just ten and gradually increase the offer as needed), depending on how good the segment was. But one hundred was the cap.

We thought we were getting a bargain since most people did agree to do it for nothing (the whole "wanna be on TV" thing), but we ended up paying for it in other ways. We left everyone with our contact information, and many of the participants would pester us by phone, usually starting on *the same day*, wanting to know when their segment was going to air. When they called, we usually didn't know ourselves. We just told them "soon."

Once enough of the on-locations were in the can, we started production on the studio segments hosted by DeLuise, which would tie them together in the edited half-hour shows. I would usually be on hand (though I wasn't doing the audience warmup) and they would have me come out and discuss the bits that I had appeared on. DeLuise would introduce me as "Our own Bob Perlow!"

Referring to an on-camera personality with the prefix "our own" is something that goes back to the early days of TV, presumably so that viewers could differentiate the regular performers from guest stars. However, it seemed a bit dated by the Nineties, and as a result it would become my nickname on the set: "Hey, 'Our Own!'" "How's it going, 'Our Own?'" "Wanna get lunch, 'Our Own?'" etc. There was one strange stagehand, Victor, who when he saw me would give me the ever-popular "I gotchyer 'Our Own' right here!" while grabbing his crotch. (*Not nice*, Victor.)

DeLuise was as nice off-camera as you would imagine (for openers, he never grabbed his crotch in front of me). Unfortunately, one aspect of what he did on camera ultimately did the show a bit of a disservice (all right, it probably killed it). While the segments were onscreen, DeLuise would talk over them, adding his own comments (Bert Convy had already done that while hosting *People Do the Craziest Things*, and look how well that show turned out).

This was intended to add extra humor to the segments but ended up just being intrusive. *Candid Camera* had always had a simplicity to it, both in spirt and execution. But DeLuise adding his own commentary bordered on spoon-feeding the home audience. However, he was a well-known personality and, on paper at least, we were lucky to have him. Thus, nobody wanted to bar him from doing this or argue with him about it.

But in the end this probably made less difference than the fact that for much of the public it was simply not *Candid Camera* without Alan Funt. Also, it had traditionally been a weekly show, so five times a week may have been overkill (though maybe not as much as when they tried to do *The Gong Show* that way).

The show ran less than a year, and since then this version has been more or less reduced to a footnote between the Funt family taking control of the franchise once again (Alan's son

Peter Funt would host at least one subsequent version) and the countless hidden-camera shows that would pop up as part of the wave of so-called "reality TV" (which essentially just means anything cheap to produce since there's no script).

Some purists probably even took issue with the fact that we rarely used the classic saying "Smile, you're on *Candid Camera*!" verbatim. It would usually be some variation, such as "Do you know you're on *Candid Camera*?" or "By the way, you're on *Candid Camera*!" All I know is that for the year that I was there, *Candid Camera* gave me plenty of reasons to smile.

Chapter Twenty

Coach

Coach was a show that was never a huge hit in the vein of, say, *Seinfeld* but nonetheless performed solidly enough in the ratings to keep it on for nine years (and just shy of two hundred episodes). I did warmup for the show during the entire run, at least off-and-on, notwithstanding side trips like my very brief, catastrophic tenure with *Home Improvement* (more on that—unfortunately—in the next chapter).

What made it a bit remarkable that the show would last nine years was the fact that the two male leads, Craig T. Nelson and Jerry Van Dyke, never got along very well. I never discovered the exact origin of their feud. In fact, if I had to guess I'd say there probably *wasn't* one. I imagine it was just the standard clash of egos (which I had seen, in one form or another, on many other shows).

But in this case, the tension was so intense that they weren't even able to hide it from the studio audience. They would go offstage in order to argue in private, but that was pointless since they would then be so loud that everyone in the studio heard them.

Nelson played the title character, football coach Hayden Fox of Minnesota State University. When the show began, most viewers probably knew Nelson best from dramatic roles in films such as *Poltergeist* and *All the Right Moves* (where he also played a football coach—guess he just looked like one). So people may not have realized that Nelson did have a background in comedy, including stand-up. For a while, he was also part of what now probably seems like a highly unlikely comedy duo, the other half being Barry Levinson, future director of *Rain Man*.

Bob with Craig T. Nelson

Bob with Jerry Van Dyke

On the other hand, most people realized that Jerry Van Dyke did have comedy in his blood. Decades earlier on *The Dick Van Dyke Show*, he had played his real brother's fictional brother, a banjo player with an odd sleepwalking disorder. But this had only been a recurring role; in his overall career, Jerry Van Dyke had sort of missed the boat.

The first boat Van Dyke missed, specifically, was the S.S. *Minnow*: he turned down the title role on *Gilligan's Island*, which of course ended up going to Bob Denver. Van Dyke also passed on the opportunity to join the cast of *The Andy Griffith Show* in the position that had been left vacant by Don Knotts.

During that period, Van Dyke instead agreed to the starring role in *My Mother the Car*, generally considered the worst TV sitcom of all time (for which all of us who were involved with *She's the Sheriff* are grateful). So since his instincts and corresponding track record were historically not that good, it probably made sense that Van Dyke stuck with *Coach* despite his continuing feud with Nelson. The bickering between the two was constant, although it rarely escalated to the point that it became truly physical or disruptive.

Rarely, but not never. I recall that at one taping, during one of the breaks, the argument between the two became so heated that Van Dyke stormed out of the studio. The hope was that he would calm down and return in relatively short order. However, after a certain amount of time had gone by, there became cause for concern.

Several of the producers had to go outside to look for him. Luckily, he hadn't gone far—he was sitting in the parking lot in his Rolls Royce. However, locating him was still something of an effort due to the fact that he had been chain-smoking with the windows rolled up, so there was so much smoke in the car that Van Dyke was rendered invisible.

At the same time, there was really no smoke screen ever created by Van Dyke, Nelson, or the producers regarding the relationship between the two stars. They openly acknowledged that it was a difficult one.

Still, some people were taken aback when witnessing it up close. We had former Notre Dame and pro football defensive tackle Bob Golic guest star on one episode in 1993. The strain between our two stars for that taping was at the level that the rest of us had become accustomed to, no worse than usual.

However, during one of the breaks Golic—six-foot-one and 250 pounds—approached me, almost timidly, to comment on how unnerving he found the whole thing to be. I told him that it was pretty much the same story week in and week out. (The experience didn't put Golic off sitcoms—starting that fall he would be a regular on *Saved by the Bell: The College Years* for that show's one and only season.)

In spite of all this, the two stars remained able to put their differences aside when it was necessary. Case in point: when it came to speaking directly to the studio audience, the entire cast of *Coach* was more cordial and open than possibly any cast I had ever worked with.

The cast also included Shelley Fabares as Christine Armstrong, the love interest for Hayden (the characters got married during season three). Like Van Dyke, Fabares had a strong connection to Sixties sitcoms, having played the oldest child on *The Donna Reed Show*.

In real life, Fabares married Mike Farrell in 1984. Farrell had joined the cast of *M*A*S*H* in 1975 as B. J. Hunnicut and remained with the show until its historic final episode in 1983. Farrell attended every last taping of *Coach*, and at every one I would introduce him to the crowd.

In fact, I had a whole shtick for doing so. At one usually random point during the night, I would say to the crowd in a soft, very serious voice: "Ladies and gentlemen, it gives me great pleasure to introduce someone I'm sure you're well aware of. He has brought many happy memories to you."

The audio guy recognized his cue, as he would start playing a very slow, bluesy version of the song "Suicide is Painless," known by the entire human race as the theme from *M*A*S*H*. Farrell was always okay with all of this, even standing up, turning around and waving as the crowd went crazy.

Bob with Mike Farrell

One time the show rented out all of Dodger Stadium for a cast party (it would have been closer to the spirit of the show to rent a football stadium, except LA hasn't had a team since 1994). Nelson would go on to spend six years on the NBC drama *Parenthood*. (It was announced in 2015 that *Coach* was going for the extra point, as Nelson and the cast would return for a revival series, but the project was stalled at the pilot. So again, *welcome to show business*.)

Craig T. Nelson and Jerry Van Dyke may not have gotten along, but in terms of my own time with *Coach*, I really have no complaints.

Chapter Twenty-One

Home Improvement

Home Improvement was one of the most successful TV sitcoms of the Nineties. I did the warmup for three tapings in 1994, and on the last of those I discovered that a better title for the show would have been *Attitude Improvement*—at least in regards to the show's star, Tim Allen.

As it often happened in my career, I was recruited from another show. Well, okay, more like stolen. In this case the "other show" was *Coach* (see chapter twenty). As much as I liked it there, I was naturally elated to have the chance to do an even bigger show. Working in TV in virtually any capacity is purely academic. Ideally you want to be associated with as high a rated show as possible as much as possible.

My first two tapings with *Home Improvement* went off, as they say, without incident. But my third and ultimately final taping was when I experienced the type of altercation with a sitcom's star that I had never had before (or since, thank the show business gods).

I was having what I would have said was one of my better nights working a studio audience. Everything was going right for me: just as I had at hundreds of other taping up until then, I felt I had struck the perfect balance between keeping the audience entertained and not allowing them to forget the main reason for their being there (i.e., the actual show). Also, keeping them primed for the next scene.

All in all, probably the perfect warmup night . . . or so I thought.

During one of the breaks somewhere at the middle-point of the taping, I was where I would usually be, in the bleachers, standing, talking into the mic and telling jokes or inviting audience participation. Of course, I wanted to be facing the audience, which meant I had my back to the show's set down below (I'll get to why that's important).

Everyone in the audience was laughing and clearly appeared to be having a good time. I was doing exactly what I was being paid to do, keeping them in a good mood. I was imagining at that point that I had found a home on *Home Improvement*, as I didn't think there was any possible way that the producers could miss how well I was doing that night.

Then suddenly, I—along with the entire audience—heard an angry voice coming from down on the set behind me.

"Hey!" a familiar voice bellowed. Everyone stopped laughing. We all looked down to the stage to see where the voice was coming from.

It was Tim Allen.

"The show's *down here*!" he said angrily, gesturing towards the stage he was standing on.

I was taken aback. I had been doing audience warmup for well over fifteen years and I had never experienced anything remotely like that. I really did not know how to react. I just made some kind of awkward quip (which I can't even recall), and then sort of kept it low-key until Allen had left the stage (i.e., when the coast was clear).

I figured that maybe Allen was just being facetious, or maybe that it had been his attempt at irony. Or he might have been simply having a bad night, like we all have every now and again.

But I got my "official" answer the very next day. I received a phone call from the line producer. He thanked me for the tapings I had already done before telling me, trying to make it seem like an afterthought: "Oh, and Tim's decided he wants to try someone else." This would be the only time I was ever fired from a warmup gig in my entire career.

I understand that performers have egos, especially comedy performers. I could have told you that going probably all the way back to my first improv try many years earlier in Boston. But Tim Allen was enjoying what would be by anyone's estimation overwhelming success in the Nineties. He had the number one show on television and was about to have success in movies (*The Santa Clause*) and even write a couple of best-selling books.

So it's hard to imagine why someone in Allen's position would feel so much concern—or, dare I say it, paranoia—about being upstaged, particularly by his warmup comic, who doesn't appear on camera and whose name doesn't appear in the credits (especially when that person's job was to make the star look good).

Just what was he afraid was going to happen, anyway? That at one point I would tell "his" studio audience, "This is lame. Let's go watch *Let's Make a Deal*!" and then they would all follow me out the door, leaving Allen and his cast to perform to an empty house?

I had already pretty much cleared a good part of my schedule in anticipation of doing more episodes of this show, and now that was out the window. Still, if what happened during that last taping was any indication of what I would have been in for if I had kept doing the show, then in hindsight I'm very glad I was forced to leave *Home* when I was.

Chapter Twenty-Two

Jay Leno and The Tonight Show

I began my thirteen years doing warmup for *The Tonight Show* in 1994. The long-running late-night talk show already had a very storied history behind it, premiering in 1954 with the legendary Steve Allen as its original host. Allen passed the reigns to Jack Paar three years later. But it was Johnny Carson's three decades as host starting in 1962 that made the show iconic and a fixture in nearly every American living room.

When I joined *Tonight*, the show was two years into Jay Leno's time as host. This was not, however, my first time crossing paths with Leno. Far from it, in fact: we already had been close friends for nearly twenty years, since long before either of us began our successful careers. We had even been roommates for a time.

I originally met Jay in Boston in 1973. We were both living there not in pursuit of comedy careers, but rather academics: Jay was a student at Emerson, working on a degree in speech therapy, while I was employed as a professor at Chamberlain Junior College (Jay is about four years younger than I am).

Suddenly, out of nowhere, someone in Boston asked us if we were funny. Not directly, but rather through an ad in the *Boston Phoenix* that put forth the very direct question: "Are you funny?" There were no further details, just the contact information. It's hard to imagine just what sort of person would respond to an ad like this, getting in touch with the party that placed it, as if to say, "Yes, I *am* funny!" But this is exactly what both Jay and I, independently of knowing each other, did.

The ad had been placed by a struggling local actor who would never go on to achieve anything noteworthy. But at the time improvisational—or improv—comedy was on the rise, thanks to The Second City and other seminal improv groups. So this guy somehow got it into his head that the city of Boston in 1974 needed to enter that particular arena.

The twenty or so people who answered the ad, including Jay and me, got together for regular practices. They were fun but didn't suggest that the project had any real potential, and it wasn't long before we reached the conclusion that the troop would never get far under the guidance of its founder. Having hit it off, Jay and I decided to break off and form our own improv troop, which we dubbed The Fresh Fruit Cocktail.

Jay and I both used the new group as a platform to hone our skills as comics, as the two of us were both still quite a ways away from being paid for performing (let alone earning a living at it). To make ends meet, Jay had a part-time job at the local Rolls Royce dealership—a fitting job for a man who would have a lifetime love for classic cars.

Jay's job, it turns out, had other perks, some of which ended up benefitting me as well. One of the vehicles on the lot was a Mercedes minibus, which he and I ended up "borrowing" on several occasions. We would drive it up and down Commonwealth Avenue and offer rides to the hitchhiking young girls who were a familiar (and for a young bachelor, *welcome*) sight on that road during that time (this was the Seventies, a seemingly more innocent time when hitchhiking was still considered safe).

During those early days in Boston, getting paid fifty dollars apiece for a single night's performance was considered a major victory. Among the bigger shows we did during that time was an opening slot for Soupy Sales, the legendary TV performer. We didn't get a chance to meet him, because he left as soon as he was done to make another gig. It was just as well: the show was at the Boston Playboy Club, so needless to say our attentions were otherwise occupied.

A year later, after leaving Emerson, Jay moved west to Los

Angeles to pursue his stand-up career. I went out there myself a short time later to become a tour guide (see chapter two), and in 1975 Jay and I decided to rent a house together in order to save money.

We found a place for rent in the central part of Los Angeles known as Los Feliz. While it's since become a trendy area populated by celebrities and punctuated by houses that have been deemed historical, at the time it was considered one of the city's less-desirable sections, just an inconsequential point between Beverly Hills and Dodger Stadium (and those houses that are now considered "historical" were only thought of as "old").

One feature that the house did have was a view of ABC Studios, where at the time they were filming *Welcome Back, Kotter* and other current sitcoms. At face value it wasn't much to look at, but it was telling for two young men who would eventually make their living in television. (Actually I had been in the facility about a year earlier—as a contestant on *The Dating Game*. In case you're wondering, yes, I lost.)

With the relatively low rent that we were paying at the time, we were able to pool our money and buy a motorcycle together. It was a 650cc 1963 Yamaha that we called "The Death Trap." The motorcycle itself was perfectly safe; it was riding them on the surrounding roads that was the potential hazard.

One day during a trip to LA's only nude beach, Pirate's Cove in Malibu, Jay declined to strip naked. This obviously would seem to defeat the whole purpose of a nude beach; however, the reason, he told me then, was that he did not want there to ever be repercussions from anyone seeing him naked after he became famous.

This incident truly reveals just how good Jay's instincts were. First of all, he knew even then that he was destined for success. But he also seemed to predict the "price of fame" that was still many years away, as this was decades before camera phones, the Internet, or national scandals involving nude pictures of celebrities that they did not intend for anyone else to see (not to mention any Kardashians, who probably would've done nude selfies if those existed at the time).

Still, back then (and maybe even now) many people would have probably assumed that Jay was simply a prude. This was an easy conclusion to draw, because for whatever reason Jay was by and large oblivious to the many vices that were accepted as routine among members of our generation in the 1970s.

It's commonly documented that Jay has never drunk alcohol or used drugs, and if you're waiting for me to dispel those stories now, you're out of luck: I've never seen him do any of those things (my own dalliances with cocaine and other drugs at the time clearly never rubbed off on him). Any participation in the sexual promiscuity that defined the era also screeched to a halt once Jay met and fell in love with a young female singer to whom he remained utterly faithful.

Even numerous trips we took to Las Vegas—Sin City itself—would not get Jay to give in to temptation. Despite this, one such trip—embarked upon a few days after the New Year in 1977—would end up taking a rather morbid turn. Jay and I had taken the trip with Budd Friedman, who was the founder and owner of the influential Improv Comedy Club in New York City.

The three of us decided to take in a Frank Sinatra show at the Sands (because that's what one does when in Vegas). Once we were settled in our seats (near the kitchen), we noticed that the best seats in the house—at a booth directly in front of the stage—were unoccupied. We assumed that whomever it was reserved for had simply changed their plans.

The closer it got to showtime, the more we started to imagine that the booth was going to remain empty. So we spontaneously decided not to let it go to waste. Why can't *we* just sit there? Having a reasonable amount of show business pull at the time, Friedman talked to the manager, who agreed that we could go ahead and upgrade ourselves to that booth.

Needless to say, we felt like the kings of Vegas sitting at the best seat in the house for a concert by the legendary performer. But shortly after the show, we found out the real story behind why the table had been vacant in the first place.

It turns out it had been reserved for Frank Sinatra's mother, Natalia. Sinatra considered her to be his good luck charm and wanted her to be at every show, so he had commissioned a private jet to bring her in for this one. That night, she ended up being killed when the small plane crashed into a mountain.

Back in Los Angeles, while Jay was continuing to hone his stand-up act he was also beginning to achieve some visibility as an actor, making appearances on sitcoms like *Good Times*, *Alice*, and *One Day at a Time*. He also had a major role on a 1979 episode of *Laverne & Shirley*, when I was both doing warmup and working as a member of the writing staff.

When he wasn't acting, much of Jay's time was spent in the LA Improv and other comedy clubs, where he ended up forming sort of a "gang" that also included *Good Times* star Jimmy Walker, as well as future comedy titans David Letterman and Jerry Seinfeld. (During those days, up-and-coming talent was truly everywhere you looked: one of the waitresses at the club was future Oscar-nominated actress Debra Winger.)

It wasn't long before Jay caught the attention of Helen Kushnick, a talent agent who was already representing Walker and other successful comedians. Kushnick recognized Jay's potential but immediately wanted him to make changes to potentially broaden his appeal, starting with his appearance. Some other "advisors" even suggested that his chin (the very chin that was later to become known the world over) be reduced surgically.

Jay refused to go under the knife (his instinct once again right on point), but he did agree to a far less drastic variance in his image, this one involving wearing a porkpie hat and smoking a pipe (it should be obvious by now that Jay was not a smoker). This attempt would also end up being short-lived.

Despite her early miscalculations, Kushnick would remain Leno's agent right up into his time as host of *The Tonight Show*. There she became an executive producer, and her ruthless tactics—supposedly all in the interest of Jay's career and the show—would result in a very public meltdown later documented in Bill Carter's book *The Late Shift*, which was adapted into an HBO movie where Kushnick was portrayed by Kathy Bates. (Her more extreme actions included placing a lifetime ban from the show on any celebrity who appeared on Letterman's new CBS show first.) Kushnick parted ways with Leno over the scandal and died in 1996.

In the interim, however, Kushnick did help Jay as he rose in popularity during the 1980s, due largely to his many appearances on *Late Night with David Letterman*. Jay then became one of several revolving guest hosts on *The Tonight Show* (following Joan Rivers's controversial departure in 1985). In 1992, it was announced that Jay would take over permanent hosting duties on the mammoth program following Johnny Carson's imminent retirement.

To be completely honest, I had been hoping—maybe even assuming—that when Jay got the *Tonight Show* gig I was a shoo-in for the audience warmup. This turned out not to be the case (it was the network's decision, not Jay's). However, based on the way the show approached their warmup after Jay took over, it was a safe bet that it would not be too long before there was an opening.

The warmup was being handled by the show's head writer, Jimmy Brogan, who would try to interact with individual audience members using predicable starting points such as where they were from (which everyone knows is not my favorite) or what they did for a living. Brogan was a stand-up comic and a nice guy. But for what was not just a major network show but one desperately trying to maintain its relevance for a new generation, Jimmy's method was a bit too low-key and lacking in energy.

This was really not doing any favors for Jay's first year at *The Tonight Show*, which was already being impaired by bad reviews and low ratings. Meanwhile, I was actually auditioning for *The Tonight Show* without even realizing it. My unprecedented success doing warmup for sitcoms had yet to carry over to talk shows. In that world, I essentially was forced to start back in the wading pool. I wanted to do warmup for *Tonight*, but it would have to be *Later*.

Later originally premiered in 1988, hosted by sportscaster Bob Costas. The show, a half-hour in length with no studio audience, aired on NBC at 1:30 a.m., presented as a marginally more "serious" offering for any viewer who was still awake after the Carson and Letterman shows.

After Costas left the show in 1994, Greg Kinnear took over as host and *Later* was revised to resemble a much more conventional late-night talk show, complete with a live studio audience. The show continued to air in its 1:30 a.m. slot, still very much late-night TV no-man's-land.

Well maybe not *no* man, but certainly few. Generally, only about nineteen people comprised the studio audience for *Later*. But in my career I always gave 100 percent at every taping, regardless of how popular a show was or how many people were in the audience (or how much I was getting paid).

Because of what I was doing, those nineteen people in the audience for *Later* were beginning to sound like about a thousand people laughing, so much so that it became impossible for *The Tonight Show* producers not to hear it from down the hall of the same studio where both shows were being taped. In 1995, I was—*finally*—offered the job as the regular warmup comic for the show.

Even after the uphill battle in landing the gig, *The Tonight Show* was quite possibly the pinnacle of my success. The show was done in a method that's known as "live to tape," which as explained earlier means that it's taped start to finish with no retakes (except for very rare occasions) as though the show were airing live.

Unlike on sitcoms, where I had to go back to interacting with the audiences during breaks in filming throughout the show, I would do warmup at the beginning of the taping and then just sit down and enjoy the show along with everyone else (unless some technical problem had to temporarily halt production, in which case I would get up and keep the audience occupied while it was being dealt with, which happened maybe once or twice a month).

I started doing the show just before Jay was starting to turn the ratings around. Ironically, while Jay has in fact never been the subject of any sort of serious personal scandal (that's what happens when you leave your swimming trunks on), it was two high-profile celebrity scandals that ended up helping him.

In 1994, former football superstar O. J. Simpson was put on trial for the murder of his ex-wife and a man named Ron Goldman—a long, drawn-out, televised trial that became completely inescapable in the media. Although nearly the entire comedy world at the time weighed in on it somehow, *Tonight* introduced an ongoing gag known as The Dancing Itos, choreographed hoofers who resembled the trial judge, Lance Ito. The concept was simple, silly, and became Jay's first high-profile talk-around-the-water-cooler recurring bit as host of *The Tonight Show*.

As perfect as the timing of The Dancing Itos may have been, it was nothing compared to what happened on the show the following year. British actor Hugh Grant had already been booked on the show to promote his new film *Nine Months*, but Jay, as well as the public, would end up getting considerably more than they bargained for—a concept that Grant himself had already experienced, to put it mildly.

Earlier that year, Grant had been arrested in LA for soliciting a prostitute. This might not seem to constitute especially outlandish behavior for a Hollywood celebrity. However, in contrast to, say, Charlie Sheen or Russell Brand, Grant's public image was generally boyish and non-threatening (say nothing of the fact that when this happened, he was supposed to have been engaged to actress Elizabeth Hurley).

Many in his position would probably have cancelled the appearance, but Grant chose to face the music. Looking clearly remorseful yet somehow relaxed, Grant came out and sat down, when just seconds into the segment Jay asked: "Let me start with question number one: What the *hell* were you thinking?"

Jay didn't pose the question as though Grant were on trial; rather, his tone suggested that he honestly wanted to get Grant's side of the story so that everyone could put the scandal behind them and laugh about. Also clearly not wanting to make the situation worse than it already was, Grant acknowledged that he'd made a mistake and apologized for his actions.

From this single TV interview, not only was Grant able to save his reputation and career, but Jay's ratings skyrocketed ("from worst to first," as they say), establishing the foundation for what would become a successful two decades on the show.

I was there for the next thirteen years until cuts in the budget sent me packing. As for Jay, while I've already talked about how good his instincts have always been, after being his close friend for forty years, I believe it's all best summed up by something he would always say about connecting with one's audience: that for every one person a performer is nice to, word of mouth will eventually gain him three hundred new fans. Being a jerk to one audience member, on the other hand, will likely ensure that eventually a thousand people will loathe him from just that one. This is what we might call "comedy math" . . . and Jay Leno is Einstein.

Chapter Twenty-Three

Friends

I did the warmup for *Friends* for its first three seasons. Nearly twenty years later, I'm still trying to figure out just whose "friends" those people were. They certainly weren't mine, or those of anyone unfortunate enough to be stuck in the studio audience. Doing that show was among the most miserable experiences of my career.

I was there from the beginning, doing warmup for the pilot in 1994. To their credit, the series did hit its stride very quickly; it takes most shows months or even a full season (or longer) to simply find itself as effortlessly as *Friends* did during that first taping. There had just been an overall feeling among everyone involved that this was something special. Once the show began airing, the ratings indicated that the public thought so, too.

The *Friends* pilot was also a fairly standard taping, which added to the false sense of security that I was then allowing myself to develop. By the third episode, however, the problems that would plague the show's tapings for the rest of its run (or at least as long as I was there) would start to become all too apparent.

By this period of TV production, the average time to tape a sitcom—which in its final edit would barely exceed twenty minutes—was about five hours. This was already pretty ridiculous.

However, *Friends* took usually as long as *eight hours* to tape.

What I always thought accounted for this was that the creators of the show, David Crane and Marta Kauffman, had only one other TV project to their credit: *Dream On*, a one-camera sitcom with no live studio audience. They'd become accustomed to taking as long as they felt like to shoot one episode, even days if they thought it was necessary.

If you're thinking, "So what's a couple of extra hours in the grand scheme of things?" you were obviously never at a *Friends* taping. Had you been, you'd know that you felt every last second of that time.

I'm sure there are some events that might warrant sitting in the same place for eight hours. Say, an outdoor music festival. But would anyone want to sit through an eight-hour music festival if it were only one band playing every song three or four times in a row—with very long breaks in between? Of course not. But this was pretty much what a *Friends* taping was akin to (plus at the festival you'd at least be allowed to get up, walk around, and get something to eat, which you couldn't even do at these tapings).

These proceedings would soon become particularly draining for me, since my job was to keep the audience occupied and entertained any time the cameras weren't rolling. Even with my background as an improv comic, I found I simply didn't have enough material to be able to go for *that* long: I felt I had used up all the words I knew, and in every combination.

As with most of the five-hour tapings, the main reason it took as long as it did was retakes. By the Nineties, we were a million miles from the way *I Love Lucy* used to film a show straight though, only stopping maybe long enough to change the scenery. Modern sitcom tapings typically were doing a lot of multiple takes, but those *were* often for legitimate reasons, such as an actor flubbing a line or some sort of technical problem.

However, on *Friends* they were never satisfied with just one take, even if that first attempt went perfectly (which it usually did). On rare occasions, I'd see them be okay with "only" two takes. But rarely fewer than three, and *never* just one.

Of course, familiarity breeds contempt, which is why the laughter coming from the studio audience dwindled with every subsequent take of the same scene or shot. Who's ever going to laugh at the same joke just as hard—if at all—when they hear it three or more times inside the span of just a few minutes?

Forced to sit through this nonsense, the audience would inevitably take out their frustration on me alone. Thinking that I was not merely the warmup guy but the audience's shepherd—if not their puppet-master—the producers somehow held me accountable for the decreased volume of laughs for those third and fourth takes. So they would always take me aside and ask me to provide some sort of explanation.

I would give them any excuse I could think of, usually something involving the sound or the lighting or both. Of course, what I longed to tell them was the truth. In spite of the show's success, how these so-called professionals were seemingly unable to grasp this concept on their own is beyond me.

Another element slowing the whole process down needlessly was the show's writers. It was not uncommon at sitcom tapings to stop the action in order to have an impromptu writers' meeting right in front of the audience, where they would "fix" a joke or scene that they suddenly realized wasn't working.

In most cases, these "new" jokes that the *Friends* writers miraculously seemed to come up with were actually leftovers from earlier in the episode's writing process; the only thing that was spontaneous (if anything) was the decision to resurrect them (i.e., "Hey, what was that joke we had on Monday that we *sort of* liked?").

Again, I'd seen this happen on other sitcoms, but only occasionally. The *Friends* writers somehow felt the need to do this at virtually every shoot! And they wouldn't stand to the side of the stage as they did this, either—they would actually sit down at the Central Perk coffee house set! I guess they really wanted everyone to think that they were geniuses for coming up with these jokes on the fly. But they weren't—coming up with the jokes on the fly *or* geniuses.

Throughout this whole debacle, one group of people I might have hoped to get at least a little bit of support from was the stars of the show: Courtney Cox, David Schwimmer, Jennifer Aniston, Matt LeBlanc, Matthew Perry, and Lisa Kudrow (who, like myself, was a veteran improv comic).

Among the many sitcoms I've been involved with, on probably nine out of ten shows the stars were willing to have some interaction with the studio audience, talking directly to them or even going out into the bleachers to mix with them a bit.

Among the *Friends* cast, the only actor I saw even occasionally acknowledge the audience was Perry, who from time to time would come out and wave or say a quick

Bob with Matt LeBlanc

"hello." Other than that, I don't remember *ever* seeing any of them try to directly connect with the people who had come to watch them. I didn't get the impression that these actors were snobs, or that they thought they were too good for the general public; just that as successful as the show was, they had no reason to bother.

Everyone seems to want to know, even still, if the members of the cast were, in fact, all friends with one another in real life. With a show that successful and six stars all vying for the spotlight on their own, you would expect there to be ego-clashing somewhere along the lines. But if there was ever any serious friction among the actors on *Friends*, I honestly never witnessed it (certainly in contrast to, say, the feud between the two male leads on *Coach*).

Then again, it's always possible I missed a few things because I would tend to have my hands quite full. My general job description primarily entailed keeping audience

The cast and crew of Friends *during its second season*

Bob on the series's iconic Central Perk couch

members in a good mood; but late in a *Friends* taping, it would inevitably become more about making sure people didn't simply walk out.

Having been doing warmup for twenty-five years at that point, I had become adept at charting the deterioration of my relationship with the audience members as a taping wore on. I had it pretty much down to a science: when we started out, I was every audience member's buddy. Around the third hour, they thought of me as just the guy standing there with the mic. By that fourth hour I was the school principal keeping them in detention, and by hour five I had become their prison warden.

So you can imagine that by the unprecedented eighth hour, these people were pretty much thinking they'd gone to hell, and that I was Satan.

Although I had had my share of experience with audience members wanting to leave before a shoot wrapped, it happened so much on *Friends* that I was forced to pull out every trick I had (and invent a few new ones in the process) to try and convince people not to go.

Whenever someone got up with the clear intention of exiting, I had no choice but to embarrass them by asking them to stay: doing so over the mic, and being sure to call everyone else's attention to what was going on. The would-be escapees frequently got very angry with me, sometimes becoming so loud that it mattered less and less that I was on mic and they weren't. Then I'd lead the crowd in a chant of "Please don't go! Please don't go!" (Although I knew that while they were chanting, most of them were actually thinking: "Go! Leave! Then maybe they'll let the rest of us go, too!")

One night I even had an audience member stand up and—acting as a representative for everyone in attendance that night—actually uttered those immortal words, "Let my people go!" (P.S. It didn't work).

I never took any pleasure in doing this, but making sure that people stayed there was part of my job. Honestly, it was better to have some tourist from Indiana or wherever shooting eye-daggers at me than have the show's producers think I wasn't capable of doing what I was being paid to do.

Another tactic I sometimes (reluctantly) employed was guilting the person into hanging around by informing them just how fortunate they were to have gotten to watch the show for free when "we" could've sold their ticket for hundreds of dollars (a complete lie). I would remind them of all those poor souls in other parts of the country who would never have the chance to see a real TV show being taped (even though I knew that the ones who never got to see this particular show being taped were actually the lucky ones).

As I understand it, some of the warmups who did *Friends*

after I did would not do as well in getting people to stay and often ended up contending with a mass exodus in those later hours. By contrast, I'm happy to say, very few people ultimately left on my watch. But it always took some doing.

On occasion, when someone absolutely insisted that they had to leave, I would tell them that I'd give them a ride to wherever they needed to go once the taping was over. Thankfully, I knew how to say this in just the right tone to make it clear that the offer was a joke, and that I was merely punctuating how important it was for them to remain there.

So—thank God—no one ever actually expected a ride from me after the show. This is a particularly good thing since I'd have been afraid to be alone in a moving vehicle with anyone who had probably just become temporarily psychotic from having sat through an entire *Friends* taping.

Not that I would have blamed anyone for becoming disgruntled. In summing up the overall way that *Friends* treated their studio audience, I always end up going back to the same word: abuse. That may seem harsh, but based on what I saw I really can't adequately describe it any other way.

Perhaps the most flagrant example I ever witnessed happened in the second season. I've come to refer to it as "The Marie Antoinette Incident." She, of course, was the Queen of France who, according to legend, said "Let them eat cake!" in response to being told that the peasants were starving.

It involved the director, Michael Lembeck. He was the son of Harvey Lembeck, who played the inept biker Eric Von Zipper in the *Beach Party* movies of the Sixties. The younger Lembeck had also been a performer: in the mid-Seventies he appeared on Saturday morning TV as lead singer of Kaptain Kool and The Kongs, a faux rock band that was sort of a hybrid of Kiss and ABBA.

Michael Lembeck is probably best known to the general public for his role of Max, the husband of Mackenzie Phillips's character on *One Day at a Time*; he would later go on to direct feature films such as *The Santa Clause 2* and *The*

Tooth Fairy. I had worked with him before *Friends*, when he had been an actor on *Foley Square*. When we did that show, I remember thinking that he was an okay guy. But on this particular day . . . not so much.

On nearly all TV and film sets, what's called in the industry "craft services" supplies food and beverages to be available for the cast and crew. Fair enough—they are *working*, after all. At most sitcom tapings, food is neither given out nor sold to the audience. However, as I've mentioned it took about eight hours to do *Friends*. And who ever goes that long without so much as a bite?

So at this second-season taping, Lembeck had a couple of his own real-life friends there to watch the show. During one of the many long (and unnecessary) breaks, he and his two cronies each went and got a full plate of food from craft services. The audience was already growing impatient, and seeing that the director was getting ready to sit and eat obviously meant that taping wasn't about to be resuming any time soon. Right off the bat, this didn't help matters any.

But that was *nothing* compared to what happened next. There were probably a half dozen places around the set where Lembeck and his buddies could have sat down and eaten without being in plain sight of the rest of the people there. Yet, for reasons that elude me to this day, they chose to sit and eat right in the middle of the audience, even knowing full well that everyone else was just as hungry as they were (if not more so).

Looking to avoid having the French Revolution (The *Friends* Revolution?) break out right then and there, I tried my best to defuse the situation the same way I did every potentially awkward situation: by making light of it. I asked Lembeck and the others (over the mic, of course): "Are we going to *share* that food?" The non-verbal response I got seemed to imply that I was the one who was being rude for interrupting their meal.

Not wanting to see occurrences like this repeat, I began pleading with the producers to have pizza delivered for the crowd during the taping. I explained to them that this was not jury duty, that these people were here by choice and that it obviously served our collective purpose to keep them in the best mood possible under the circumstances.

Finally, by the third season, they complied and the studio audience got their pizzas. But I still don't think it should've taken that much effort on my part. (It's fitting that Lembeck would eventually direct *The Tooth Fairy*, because the whole process was like pulling teeth.)

But pizza only goes so far. Not surprisingly, with everything that was going on, in three years I very, *very* rarely saw any of the same faces in the audience at more than one taping. Little matter, since the series almost never had any trouble filling all the seats. Given its immense popularity, every plane bringing tourists in from Middle America meant fresh victims for this slow torture.

Of course, none of the travesties I've been describing would ever end up on the air: through the eternal magic of editing, the final show would always end up smelling like roses (and share points). At least this is what I assume: *Friends* was one of the few shows I worked on that I could never bring myself to actually watch. The whole experience on the set just completely soured it for me.

So you're probably wondering, given my list of grievances with *Friends*, what could have possessed me to stay there for three years? No, I wasn't contractually obligated; as with most of the shows I did, I only agreed to one taping at a time. Actually my motivation was very simple: money. Even doing as well as I was by then, *Friends* paid me about a third more than other shows did. So I guess when all is said and done, I'm just as guilty as anyone else.

But after those three seasons, I felt like no amount of money could have kept me around, at least not week in and week out. I did come back a couple of times after, just to fill in.

One of the later episodes that I did end up doing featured Brad Pitt as the guest star. At the time, Pitt was married to

Jennifer Aniston, and the episode's premise was sort of an inside joke: he played an old acquaintance of the group who didn't like Aniston's character. Life, it seems, would imitate art when they got divorced in 2005.

Even though he was a huge movie star, Pitt was actually quite directly cordial towards the studio audience—far more so than I ever saw any of the regular cast members being! The crowd, in turn, naturally loved not only Pitt but the attention that he was willing to bestow upon them.

While this was going on, I starting thinking that maybe this *Friends* taping would finally be different, that because Pitt was there everyone would be willing to stay until it was actually completely finished, and I would be relieved from at least that particular burden.

Wrong again! It turns out that even Brad Pitt isn't enough to keep people at a sitcom taping for eight grueling hours. I was right back to trying to verbally wrestle people back into their seats as they attempted to flee.

Once again, I was reminded of why I had made the decision to stop doing the show regularly. This ended up being my last time with this sitcom, and as far as I was concerned, it was good riddance to bad *Friends*.

Chapter Twenty-Four

Scare Tactics

Scare Tactics was yet another hidden camera show, but no, I did not appear on-screen to set stunts up as I had on *People Do the Craziest Things* and *Candid Camera*. This one involved filming the reactions of people who end up in scenarios that might be out of a horror movie. I was involved with the show for a total of only a couple of hours, but in that time it still managed to scare *me*, inadvertently.

Scare Tactics premiered in 2003 on Sci-Fi Channel (which was renamed Syfy in 2009) and featured introduction segments that were usually filmed in the studio without a live audience. However, they were doing a retrospective, a "best-of" episode, and decided to break formula a bit with a location shoot.

They set up the elevated stage at the busy tourist attraction Universal CityWalk in Hollywood. A crowd of fans had gathered to watch, and I had been hired to do more or less what I would have done in a studio: provide introductions, interact with the audience, give t-shirts away, etc. The crowd consisted mostly of younger men who were there to get a look at the show's host, Shannen Doherty.

The actress had become popular as the star of two prime-time dramas, *Beverly Hills, 90210* and *Charmed*. She was also known for diva-like behavior and very public meltdowns, which got her fired from both shows. (The only thing I can really weigh in on there is that supposedly on the latter series she got along very badly with costar Alyssa Milano. I have some difficulty comprehending this after working with Milano for two years on *Who's the Boss?*, knowing how extremely personable and professional she is.)

But apparently getting busted down to being the host of a reality show on a relatively small cable network didn't humble Doherty a whole lot. I was supposed to be there for only about ten minutes before she came out, and that turned into an hour and a half. From what they were telling me, she was refusing to come out of her trailer—and holding up the whole shoot in the process. The producer at one point just sighed as he told me matter-of-factly, "We're used to this."

Spending thirty-five years on television and saying you've never witnessed egos being disruptive would be like being in the navy for that long and claiming you'd never seen water. But being pretty much accustomed to egos didn't mean I liked having to deal with them.

Doherty finally came out, to the enthusiastic (but as far as I was concerned undeserved) cheering of her crowd of admirers. This meant I was now done with what I had been hired to do for the afternoon. I thanked them and walked away, not looking back. Oh, and *here's* a shockingly unexpected twist worthy of any hidden camera show: Doherty was fired from *Scare Tactics* during the next season.

Chapter Twenty-Five

Dharma & Greg

For the second half of my audience warmup career, starting in the early Nineties, one thing I would do at tapings was make prank calls. I realize the idea was hardly original: on the radio, every Howard Stern wannabe in even the smallest markets was doing them, and a couple of guys—The Jerky Boys—even made a whole career out of it.

Still, prank calls, if properly executed, had the potential to be very funny. I did them at every taping and used the same setup, because it almost always produced entertaining results. The concept was just a little bit shocking, maybe even dangerous, as we were now in the final few years of the twentieth century and nobody had Prince Albert in a can anymore (they finally let him out so that he wouldn't suffocate).

But what was surprising about the prank call that I would end up doing at dozens of tapings was 1) the precise sitcom on which the routine ended up getting censored and 2) the person who would blow the whistle on me.

This was the show: *Dharma & Greg*, which premiered in the fall of 1997. The premise involved a lawyer (played by Thomas Gibson, who to this day has not smiled on *Criminal Minds*) from a snooty upper-crust background and a yoga instructor (Jenna Elfman) who was raised by hippies. The titular characters decide to get married on a whim after one date. It was also one of the earlier shows created and produced by Chuck Lorre, who would go on to huge success with *Two and a Half Men* and *The Big Bang Theory*.

Got all that? Okay, now this was the prank:

I would start out by asking for a willing participant, who

would have to be a girl—at least eighteen years old—who was from out-of-town and not traveling with her parents. She would also have to be relatively certain that at least one of her parents (or, alternately, grandparents) would be home to answer a phone call.

What was going to happen once we made the call was that the girl would have the chance to win not just a t-shirt but also a souvenir cap (yeah, we *really* broke the bank on this one). All she would have to do was successfully convince her parent to let her participate in a dance contest, which she would say was for a five hundred dollar prize.

Oh, er, um . . . one more thing . . . This was to be a *topless* dance contest.

The stagehands would bring out the phone, which was already rigged so that the other end of the call would be come out of the speakers for everyone to hear it. The girl would then dial the number (this would always be even better if the people were woken up out of bed for this, so I looked for East Coast or Midwest participants, trying to time it accordingly by taking the time zones into account).

Once we had the parent (or grandparent) on the line, the girl would set it up by telling them that they hadn't been able to get into the TV taping so they decided to go to a club instead. This is where I usually took over: they handed the phone over to me. Then I would assume my character, the sleazy club owner with the obligatory Brooklyn accent (even though I was calling from the one of the furthest points, geographically, from Brooklyn in the United States).

I identified myself as the owner of an . . . um . . . "establishment"—a "gentleman's club," if you will—called Bob's Classy Ladies. I would tell them that their daughter had a chance to win a five hundred dollar prize and that even though she was over eighteen there was some obscure California law (which I made up) that still made verbal parental consent by phone necessary if the girls even looked a little underage.

Then I would find a way to casually slip the word "topless"

into the conversation, just slyly (borderline subliminally) enough for them to catch it. Needless to say, this always got their attention. Often these girls would be traveling with their girlfriends, and I would drop those names too in order to give the whole thing further credibility.

Then I drove it home: we started playing the song "You Can Leave Your Hat On" by Joe Cocker, and I told the parents that their daughter was already onstage and well into her "dance," reacting as though I were watching it. I even got the entire audience in on it, cueing them to whoop and holler to stimulate the crowd at the "club" watching this girl doing her thing topless. I'd tell the parent that I mistakenly heard them say "yes" to their daughter doing this.

Actually, about thirty percent of the time, they would give permission (albeit reluctantly), saying that their daughter was an adult and could make her own decisions, or that they trusted her judgment, or something along those lines.

The rest of the time, however, they would completely lose it and scream bloody murder at me, often including threats to sue me and the "club" or send the police (as more and more people had caller ID, sometimes we would hear from the police on the same line minutes later).

Once the call was finished, I would send the girl out into the hall to call her parents right back to explain what had just happened and let them off the hook. Not once did anyone we called seem to suspect that it was all a joke (at some tapings I would do this whole thing twice, with two different girls).

However, during my sixth taping of *Dharma & Greg*, I ended up getting a bit of a surprise that *I* had not been expecting. I was well into the prank call, and it was going well, as it almost always did. Suddenly, Jenna Elfman came out on stage and got on the mic.

"What are you doing!" she said angrily. "You're scaring people!" I don't know if she hadn't noticed what I was doing at previous tapings or if that night was just the last straw. Either way, she demanded that we hand the phone over to her.

She spoke into it, and the beginning of the verbal exchange

went something like this (keep in mind, the entire audience could still hear both ends of the conversation):

ELFMAN: Hi. This is Jenna Elfman. I just wanted to . . .
PARENT: Who?
ELFMAN: You know, Jenna Elfman. I'm the star of *Dharma & Greg*.
PARENT: *Who?* Sorry, I'm not familiar with your show.

She appeared crestfallen that this person apparently didn't know who she was . . . even though it was entirely possible that someone in Middle America who's old enough to have a grown daughter might not know who Jenna Elfman is. I'm not assuming anyone is a "hick" (I'm from the middle of nowhere myself), but rather that people have lives that don't always allow them to keep up with every single popular TV show, movie, or music act (even if they wanted to).

Yet Elfman was clearly more offended by my phone routine than by this person not being able to identify her, because she still went ahead with apologizing to the person for my actions and telling them it wasn't right for anyone to use their child to frighten them in that way. In my defense, all of the girls who participated enjoyed the bit, as did the people we phoned once it was explained to them. Not to mention the girls all walked away with a smile—and one remarkably cool souvenir hat.

Finally, they had to take the phone away from the star, and that was the end of the bit, at least as far as this one show was concerned. It's sort of odd that Elfman, whose character was defined by being a "free spirit," would suddenly elect herself as the show's one-woman vice squad. After that I would do *Dharma & Greg* another six times . . . but without the prank call.

Looking back, I probably have to agree that the bit was, at the very least, in questionable taste. And was it risky? Maybe. Was it crude? A little. Was it funny? Yes to that as well. And that was the whole point of my being there (plus *everyone* loved it—other than Jenna Elfman).

Chapter Twenty-Six

The Wrapup Guy

If you're of a certain age, you may remember a time when it was customary on a game show to give away something that they called the "home version." This was a portable game based on the show that usually came in a small cardboard box and was also commercially available at toy stores. Often shows would give one away to each person who appeared on the program (as part of what they used to call "lovely parting gifts") so that everyone could have the fun of playing *Jeopardy!* or *Password* in their living room.

Accordingly, I've come up with a "home version" of being a warmup comic, which has always been what I suggest to people if they want to understand what my job was typically like. It's actually a far more complex version of the children's party game musical chairs: what you want to do is set up eight chairs in your living room facing the TV. Invite eight friends over and seat them in the chairs. Put a DVD of any TV sitcom on and play one episode.

Now here's the object of the game: see if you can get them all to stay in those seats for about five hours. During that time, you'll play the DVD, but only individual scenes. Then play the exact same scene over again. And *again*. And *one more time* if you want the real experience. And then shut the DVD off for, say, twenty minutes.

When the DVD is not on, you need to try to find things to occupy them. Tell jokes, ask them questions, start sing-alongs, anything that'll keep them in those seats. Oh, and did I mention while those people are sitting there for those five hours, they can't eat or drink anything?

The good news is they can go to the bathroom. But only if escorted by someone (so you'll need an additional participant for that role).

And if you're successful, what do you win? Why, a chance go through the whole thing again a week later, of course! (Or if you want to play the advanced version, try going through this three or four times a week.)

If you've read this far, then hopefully you're not one of the people I would need to urge to take this challenge (so you can tell your eight friends to make other plans). Yet I have always found myself up against people who essentially thought I was just an "announcer," that I could have just been reading off train schedules out over the PA system at Grand Central Station.

This is not to suggest that I've never gotten any appreciation or recognition beyond just my income. During my years in Hollywood I occasionally would be recognized on the streets, and then people would ask for autographs or want me to pose for a picture with them (I always complied).

Okay, at two or three times a week this probably happened to me less frequently than, say, Paul Newman. Or even "Newman" from *Seinfeld*. But it didn't happen to me enough for me to ever find it intrusive.

There have been comparatively few times that I've been recognized for the work I did onscreen, because if you've read this far you also know that there never was all that much of that. I thoroughly enjoyed the work I got to do on camera and definitely would have had liked the chance to do more (or more specifically, I would have liked it if some of my on-camera efforts had been more successful).

My career has not come without a price. Several years ago I began having trouble with my hearing and had to see a specialist, who confirmed that I was indeed suffering from permanent hearing loss. He asked what I had done as a career, and once I told him he instantly said that this explained it. It was a result of thirty-five years in close proximity to a crowd of three hundred people simultaneously making noise (and the irony is, part of my job was to make sure they made as much noise as possible). Still, if I had to have my hearing damaged, I'm glad it was this way and not from decades of working a jackhammer.

What I've done may have contributed to the way live sitcoms are taped, but not necessarily in a way that's all positive. Obviously I've been a bit critical of the producers of *Friends* and other shows that end up taking as much as eight hours to film a (not even) half-hour sitcom. But in all fairness, it may be a chicken-or-egg situation: Do these shows take longer to film because guys like me—career warmup comics—were available, or did our availability, and with it the knowledge that we'd keep the audience in their seats for however long, become (or at least contribute to) the reason the tapings took longer and longer?

At the same time, there've been fewer and fewer shows that use a live studio audience. The rise of single-camera sitcoms like *The Office, Modern Family,* and *Girls* has altered the sitcom landscape considerably, and some say that live-audience sitcoms—and by extension warmup comics—are an endangered species.

Of course, they (have we ever figured out who "they" are?) also once said that the laugh track was going to make studio audiences for sitcoms obsolete until shows like *All in the Family* and *Mary Tyler Moore* brought them back stronger than ever.

So who knows what the future holds for TV comedy or the practice of audience warmup? Maybe they'll invent a hologram of a comedian that will be capable of doing it and programmed for every eventuality. The downside would be that if anyone tried to leave a taping because it dragged on for too long, they would simply be able to walk right through the warmup guy.

I have an idea about my own immediate future, at least. I've also been having some success with a one-man show I put together based on all my many experiences entitled Tales from Hollywood.

Bob on stage during his Tales from Hollywood show

Earlier, I had been using humor to make a point when I wrote that Garry Marshall spoke in a difficult-to-understand shorthand. Marshall was in fact a very intelligent and insightful man. He once said something else that has always stuck with me: "Life is more important than show business."

With that in mind, I've moved back to Rhode Island, near where my whole family still lives. I don't think I could make a bigger understatement than to say that it's different from Hollywood.

Oh, wait, I *can* think of a bigger understatement. It would be when people ask me if I know how lucky I've been in my life and career. The answer is always the same, and it's quick and it's honest: *you bet I do!*

Acknowledgments

Thanks are due to the following for their help along the way: Bob and Mickey Humphrey, the Gordon Family, the Mowrys, Sheila Perlow, Deb Anson, Garry Marshall, Ronny Marshall, Mike Borassi, Chris Cluess, Jeff Franklin, Jason Alexander, Jay Leno, Fred and Mary Willard, Alan Thicke,

Bob with Fred Willard

Bob with good friend Jay Leno

Harry Anderson, Ken Levine, Andy Aaron, Steve Forrest, the Leiweke Family, Gene Braunstein, Allan Murray, Betty, Brad Axelrod, Jeff Schmidt, and Cork & Stogie in Key West. —B. P.

Thank you to my parents, Richard John Cummins Sr. and Diane Cummins, for all their help and support. —R. J. C

Index

3rd Rock from the Sun, 95
9 to 5, 73-74

ABBA, 212
Air Bud, 131
Airplane!, 46
Alexander, Jason, 158, 161
Alice, 199
Allen, Steve, 195
Allen, Tim, 191-93
Alley, Kirstie, 77
All in the Family, 79, 225
All the Right Moves, 185
American Werewolf in London, An, 82
America's Funniest Home Videos, 126
Anderson, Harry, 97, 99-102
Andy Griffith Show, The, 154, 187
Angie, 45-48, 51
Aniston, Jennifer, 208, 215
A-Team, The, 140
Austin, Karen, 101
Avalon, Frankie, 132

Bacharach, Burt, 85-87

Back to the Beach, 133
"Bad Moon Rising," 132
Ball, Lucille, 18, 100
Bambi Meets Godzilla, 105
Barney Miller, 99
Bates, Kathy, 200
Beach Boys, The, 132
Beach Party, 212
Beatles, The, 31, 132
Bennett, Tony, 149
Berle, Milton, 18
Beverly Hills, 90210, 217
Bewitched, 78
Big Bang Theory, The, 219
Binder, Mike, 71
Blankman, 71
Blazing Saddles, 91
Bob Newhart Show, The, 79, 87, 89
Bosom Buddies, 83, 91, 126
Boston Phoenix, 195
Boston Red Sox, 95
Brady Bunch, The, 133
Brand, Russell, 202
Braunstein, Gene, 39-40, 138, 140, 144, 165
Brogan, Jimmy, 200
Brooks, James L., 71

Brooks, Mel, 91
Buddy (dog), 131
Bull and Finch (bar), 74
Bure, Valeri, 128
Burrows, James, 73

Calendar Girl Murders, 114
Callau, Tanya, 123
Cameron, Candace, 128
Cameron, Kirk, 121-22, 128
Candid Camera, 105, 110, 173-75, 182-84, 217
Cannonball Run, The, 106
Car 54, Where Are You?, 161
Carlin, George, 116
Carsey, Marcy, 91
Carsey-Werner Productions, 95
Carson, Johnny, 113, 195, 200-201
Carter, Bill, 200
Carvey, Dana, 148
Casino, 19
Caveman, 73
CBS This Morning, 126
Celebrity Fit Club, 151
Chamberlain Junior College, 20, 195
Charles, Glenn, 73
Charles, Les, 73
Charo, 151
Chase, Chevy, 117-18, 120, 148
Cheers, 73-79, 100, 134
Clark, Dick, 105, 172
Clooney, George, 158

Coach, 185, 187-89, 191, 209
Cochran, Johnny, 128
Cocker, Joe, 221
Comic Relief, 57
Connery, Sean, 133
Convy, Bert, 106, 183
Cops, 182
Cosby, 95
Cosby, Bill, 95
Cosby Show, The, 78, 95, 105, 108-10, 138, 173
Costas, Bob, 201
Coulier, Dave, 126, 134
Cox, Courtney, 208
Crane, Bob, 150
Crane, David, 205
Cream, 20
Creedence Clearwater Revival, 132
Criminal Minds, 219
Cruise, Tom, 150
Crystal, Billy, 57

Dallas, 88
Danson, Ted, 73, 77-78
Danza, Tony, 71, 137-38, 140-45
Darin, Bobby, 166
Dating Game, The, 197
Dawber, Pam, 54, 57
Death of a Salesman, 56
DeLuise, Dom, 151, 174, 182-83
DeVito, Danny, 67
Dharma & Greg, 219, 221-22

Dick Van Dyke Show, The, 187

"Diner, The" (*Laverne & Shirley* episode), 38

Doherty, Shannen, 217

Donna Reed Show, The, 188

Doocy, Steve, 143, 147-50, 152-53

Dorf, Larry, 161

Dream On, 206

Dreams, 128

Dr. Pepper, 82-83

Duffy, Julia, 81

Duffy, Patrick, 88

Dylan, Bob, 20

Easterbrook, Leslie, 42

Edmonton Oilers, 116

Ed Sullivan Show, The, 18

E/R (sitcom), 158

ER (drama), 158

Evan Almighty, 161

Evert, Chris, 117

Everybody Loves Raymond, 46

Fabares, Shelley, 188

Family Ties, 76, 78, 121, 138

Farrell, Mike, 188

Fogerty, John, 132

Foley Square, 213

Fonda, Jane, 112

Forrest Gump, 171

Forrest, Steve, 151

Four Seasons, The, 166

Four Tops, The, 166

Fox and Friends, 152

Fox, Fred Jr., 37

Franklin, Jeff, 125, 128, 130, 134

Frann, Mary, 82

Freed, Alan, 172

Fresh Fruit Cocktail, The, 196

Friedman, Budd, 198

Friends, 205-15, 225

Fuller House, 135

Full House, 18, 125-26, 128, 130-32, 134-35

Funicello, Annette, 18, 132

Funt, Alan, 173-74, 183

Funt, Peter, 184

Galán, Nely, 151

General Hospital, 128

Gilligan's Island, 187

Girls, 225

Gleason, Jackie, 18

Godfather Part II, The, 34

Godfather, The, 111

Goldberg, Whoopi, 57

Goldman, Ron, 202

Golic, Bob, 188

Goodtime Girls, 83

Good Times, 40, 199

Gordy, Berry, 172

Gore, Al, 49

Gorme, Eydie, 87

Grace Under Fire, 95

Graham, Bill, 168

Grammer, Kelsey, 77

Grant, Hugh, 202-4

Graves, Peter, 150

Green Acres, 161
Gretzky, Wayne, 116-17
Growing Pains, 113-15, 121, 128
Gutenberg, Steve, 125

Hair, 42
Hanks, Tom, 83
Happy Days, 31, 37, 42, 49, 54, 91
Harrelson, Woody, 77
Hartman, Phil, 148
Hayes, Robert, 46
Heaven's Gate, 113
Hello, Larry, 76
Helmond, Katherine, 85, 140-41
Hendrix, Jimi, 20
Hero at Large, 106
Hill Street Blues, 76
Hirsch, Judd, 67, 71
Hogan's Heroes, 150
Holmes, Jennifer, 81
Home Improvement, 185, 191-92
Honeymooners, The, 142
House Party with Steve Doocy, 143-44, 147-50, 152-53, 157-58, 161, 163, 165, 171, 174
Howard, Ron, 73
How the Grinch Stole Christmas!, 75
Hurley, Elizabeth, 202
Hustler, 120

I Love Lucy, 142, 206

Improv Comedy Club, 198
Indian Summer, 71
It's Garry Shandling's Show, 125

Jackass, 156
James, Kevin, 180
Jerky Boys, The, 219
Jetsons, The, 144
Joplin, Janis, 20
"Just a Gigolo/I Ain't Got Nobody," 98

Kahn, Madeline, 91-92, 94-95
Kampmann, Steven, 81
Kauffman, Martha, 205
Kaufman, Andy, 71
Kemp, Barry, 88
King of Queens, The, 180
Kinison, Sam, 116
Kinks, The, 166
Kinnear, Greg, 201
Kiss, 212
Klemperer, Otto, 150
Klemperer, Werner, 150
Klugman, Jack, 128
Knotts, Don, 187
"Kokomo," 132
Krum, Texas, 153
Kudrow, Lisa, 208
Kushnick, Helen, 199-200

LA Kings, 116
Lander, David L., 36
Larroquette, John, 100-101
Late Night with David

Letterman, 62, 166, 169, 200

Later, 201

Late Shift, The, 200

Laverne & Shirley, 31-33, 36-40, 42-43, 45-46, 51, 54, 125, 167, 199

Lawrence, Steve, 87

LeBlanc, Matt, 208

Lebowitz, Fran, 169-71

Lembeck, Harvey, 212

Lembeck, Michael, 212-14

Leno, Jay, 9, 21, 40, 195-200, 202-4

"Let Bob Do It" (*House Party* segment), 147, 149, 152-53, 157, 160, 163, 165

Let Bob Do It (TV show), 158, 161

Let's Make a Deal, 193

Letterman, David, 113, 148-49, 166, 199-201

Levy, Bob, 152

Light, Judith, 138

Linkletter, Art, 147

Live with Regis and Kathy Lee, 147

Lloyd, Christopher, 67

Long, Shelley, 73, 77

Loring, Gloria, 114

Lost in the Funhouse, 71

Loughlin, Lori, 133

Love Boat, The, 21, 106

Lundgren, Dolph, 117

"Mack the Knife," 168

Magnum, P. I., 105, 108

Makin' It, 82

Mamet, David, 105

Manson, Charles, 134

Marinaro, Ed, 42

Marjoe Gortner Tennis Tournament, 117

Marshall, Garry, 35-37, 46, 49, 54, 82, 226

Marshall, Penny, 35-36

Marx, Harpo, 88

Mary Tyler Moore (television show), 71, 73, 79, 161, 225

M*A*S*H, 42, 188

McMahon, Ed, 85, 105

Mekka, Eddie, 42

Miami Vice, 128

Mickey Mouse Club, The, 18

Milano, Alyssa, 138, 217

Milli Vanilli, 86

Minority Report, 71

Mission: Impossible, 150

Modern Family, 225

Moll, Richard, 102

Mork & Mindy, 54-58, 62-64, 73, 82, 91

Murray, Bill, 100

Myers, Mike, 148

My Mother the Car, 187

My Sister Sam, 83

National Lampoon's Vacation, 117

Naughton, David, 82-83

Nelson, Craig T., 185, 187, 189

Neuwirth, Bebe, 77
Newhart, 79, 81-83, 85, 87-90, 100, 102
Newhart, Bob, 79-82, 84-87, 89, 91, 94
Newland, Marv, 105
Newton, Wayne, 115
"New York, New York," 84, 86
New York Times, 49
Nick at Nite, 161
Nickelodeon, 161, 163
Night Court, 97, 99-101, 103-4, 150
Night of the Comet, 111-12
Night Shift, 73
Nine Months, 202

O'Donnell, Rosie, 151
Office, The, 225
Off the Wall, 53, 56-57
Oh, Madeline, 91, 94-95
Olsen, Ashley, 130-31
Olsen, Mary-Kate, 130-31
One Day at a Time, 199, 212
One Flew Over the Cuckoo's Nest, 67
Our World, 109

Paar, Jack, 195
Papenfuss, Tony, 88
Parenthood, 189
Paul Blart: Mall Cop, 180
People Do the Craziest Things, 105-6, 108-10, 138, 143, 167, 173-75, 183, 217

Perry, Matthew, 208
Pescow, Donna, 46
Phillips, Mackenzie, 212
Phillips, Sam, 172
"Pinball Wizard," 168
Pink Lady, 76
Pintauro, Danny, 138
Pitt, Brad, 214-15
Platters, The, 166
Playboy, 120-21
Playboy Mansion, 120
Pleshette, Suzanne, 89
Polar Bear Club, 156
Poltergeist, 185
Poseidon Adventure, The, 51
Posey, John, 126
Posey, Tyler, 126
Poston, Tom, 81
Presley, Elvis, 128
Producers, The, 134
Prudhomme, Paul, 151

Rain Man, 185
Raitt, Bonnie, 165
Rickles, Don, 85
Ripley's Believe It or Not, 109
Rivers, Joan, 200
Roberts, Doris, 46
Robinson, Charles, 101
Rockwell, Norman, 33
Rocky, 117, 137
Rolling Stone, 171
Roseanne, 95
Ross, Diana, 165-66, 168, 170

Roth, David Lee, 98
Ruth, Babe, 59

Saget, Bob, 126, 128, 134
Sales, Soupy, 196
Sand, Barry, 148, 151
Sanderson, William, 82, 87
Sanford and Son, 79
Santa Clause 2, The, 212
Santa Clause, The, 193
Saturday Night Fever, 46
Saturday Night Live, 76, 80, 100, 117, 148, 171
Saved by the Bell: The College Years, 188
Scaggs, Boz, 166, 170
Scare Tactics, 217-18
Schwimmer, David, 208
Scolari, Peter, 83-84, 102
Second City, The, 196
Seinfeld, 158, 161, 185, 224
Seinfeld, Jerry, 199
Shaffer, Paul, 149, 166, 169-71
Sheen, Charlie, 202
She's the Sheriff, 138, 187
Silverman, Fred, 75
Silverman, Gayle, 151-52
Simon and Garfunkel, 165-66
Simpson, O. J., 202
Simpsons, The, 71
Sinatra, Frank, 85-86, 142-43, 198-99
Sinatra, Natalia, 199
Soap, 91, 141
Somers, Suzanne, 138

Sotkin, Marc, 32-34, 43
Spector, Phil, 166
Springsteen, Bruce, 165-66, 170
Stallone, Sylvester, 137
Stamos, John, 128, 132-34
Starr, Ringo, 31, 73
Star Wars, 73
St. Elsewhere, 76
Stripes, 100
Stunt Rock, 111
Supertrain, 76
Sweetin, Jodie, 128-29

Tammy, 161
Tate, Sharon, 134
Taxi, 66, 72-73, 91, 137
Taylor, James, 165-66
Teen Wolf, 126
Telemundo, 151
Terms of Endearment, 71
Thicke, Alan, 10, 113-17, 120-21, 123
Thicke, Carter, 121
Thicke of the Night, 113
Thicke, Robert, 115
Thompson, Chris, 34
Three Men and a Baby, 125
Tolleson, Gina, 121
Tonight Show, The, 64-65, 113, 171, 195, 199-202
Tooth Fairy, The, 213-14
Tormé, Mel, 103-4, 150
Towering Inferno, The, 51
Townshend, Pete, 171
Trump, Donald, 149
TV Guide, 39, 88

TV's Bloopers and Practical Jokes, 105
Twilight Zone, The, 115
Two and a Half Men, 219

U2, 165-66
University of Rhode Island, 19-20, 47
Unusually Thicke, 123
Upside of Anger, The, 71

Valerie, 129
Van Dyke, Dick, 187
Van Dyke, Jerry, 185, 187-89
vaudeville, 56
Venice Beach, 32, 48
Voldstad, John, 88, 100

Waiting for Guffman, 93
Walker, Jimmy "J. J.," 39, 199
Weathers, Carl, 117
Weege, Reinhold, 99
Weekly World News, The, 151
Welcome Back, Kotter, 197

Werner, Tom, 91
Who's the Boss?, 71, 80, 137-38, 140-42, 145, 173, 217
Who, The, 165-66, 171
Williams, Barry, 133
Williams, Billy Dee, 149
Williams, Cindy, 35-36, 42
Williams, Robin, 32, 53-57, 59, 62-64, 91
"Will You Love Me Tomorrow," 168
Wilson, Brian, 132
Winger, Debra, 199
Winkler, Henry, 31
Winters, Jonathan, 58-63

You Again?, 128
"You Can Leave Your Hat On," 221
Young Frankenstein, 91
Young, Robert, 114
"You Really Got Me," 168

Zehme, Bill, 71